Traumas and Triumphs

"When more professionals are open and vulnerable about their own experiences with trauma and recovery, we will begin to see real change in our field and in the world in general. I applaud Dr. Foxman for his willingness to do just that, using the vehicle of his own memoir to educate. *Traumas and Triumphs* is a beautiful sharing of lived experience and life review, and I am certain that it will enhance our understanding of trauma and sharpen our skill sets for how to survive and thrive in spite of or even because of it."

—Jamie Marich, PhD, LPCC-S, LICDC-CS, REAT, RYT-500, founder of the Institute for Creative Mindfulness, author of *Trauma and the 12 Steps* and *Healing Addiction with EMDR Therapy: A Trauma-Focused Guide*

"*Traumas and Triumphs* is a compassionately-told and inspiring memoir of challenge, courage and resilience. Paul Foxman's powerful story of transforming adversity into success, meaning and true joy shines as a beacon of hope for anyone who struggles. His secrets for happiness, wise insights and compelling story make for a gripping read."

—Celeste DiMilla, psychotherapist and author of *Live Kind, Be Happy*

"Dr. Foxman is the living proof that encourages readers, especially if they have a troubled start in life, to always take the risk for growth, despite the possibility of failure. And he assures his readers those risks we find in our own lives are the path worth taking and, if we allow others to point the way or take our hand, it may not seem so scary to move toward happiness."

—Dr. Margaret Wehrenberg, author of *The 10 Best-Ever Anxiety Management Techniques*

"[Dr. Foxman] makes the case for using the pain of trauma for living a ful-filled and meaningful life. He reveals that his trauma history became 'the driving force for making the most of my life' . . . In addition to providing a vision and a sense of hope for the possibility of genuine healing from trauma and other afflictions, he provides practical guidance about how that can be achieved using the key ingredients from his 'personal recipe for happiness.'"

—Dan Collier, *Conversations for Caring*

"Dr. Foxman is an accomplished clinician, author and teacher. In *Traumas and Triumphs*, he shares his life story in an honest and powerful manner. With keen attention to detail, he describes painful experiences, professional challenges and personal success and achievements. The result is a compel-ling narrative of hope and resiliency with insight and lessons for all."

—David Fassler, MD, Clinical Professor of Psychiatry,
Larner College of Medicine, University of Vermont

"*Traumas and Triumphs* is a wild ride through Foxman's baby boomer's expe-riences, tinged with insights from a difficult New York City childhood to the turbulent '60s while training as a psychologist in many locations and settling in New England as a leader in his field. The book illuminates the author's honesty and introspection, and reveals a life of service to others."

—Michael Kerman, MSW, Leading Edge Seminars, Toronto

Traumas and Triumphs

Traumas and Triumphs

A Psychologist's Personal Recipe for Happiness

Paul Foxman, PhD

TURNER
PUBLISHING COMPANY

Turner Publishing Company
Nashville, Tennessee
www.turnerpublishing.com

Traumas and Triumphs: A Psychologist's Personal Recipe for Happiness

Cover design: Grace Cavalier
Book design: Tim Holtz

Library of Congress Cataloging-in-Publication Data
Names: Foxman, Paul, author.
Title: Traumas and triumphs : a psychologist's personal recipe for
  happiness / Paul Foxman.
Description: Nashville, Tennessee : Turner Publishing Company, [2022] |
  Identifiers: LCCN 2021030583 (print) | LCCN 2021030584 (ebook) | ISBN
  9781684428250 (hardcover) | ISBN 9781684428243 (paperback) | ISBN
  9781684428267 (ebook)
Subjects: LCSH: Foxman, Paul. | Adult child sexual abuse victims--United
  States--Biography. | Male sexual abuse victims--United
  States--Biography. | Psychologists--United States--Biography. | Psychic
  trauma--Treatment.
Classification: LCC RC569.5.A28 F68 2022 (print) | LCC RC569.5.A28
  (ebook) | DDC 616.85/83690092 [B]--dc23/eng/20211015
LC record available at https://lccn.loc.gov/2021030583
LC ebook record available at https://lccn.loc.gov/2021030584
Printed in the United States of America

Table of Contents

Acknowledgments

I wish to acknowledge all the angels who have entered my life and helped me on my journey from traumas to triumphs, often without knowing what a difference they have made. The list includes track coaches, academic advisers, therapists, vocal coaches, colleagues, interns, clients, family, guy friends, and girlfriends. These angels have made me feel worthy and lovable, and they have enhanced my self-esteem and empowered me to make my dreams come true. There are too many to thank by name and some are no longer alive, but a few stand out as particularly influential. They include Marty Spielman, Jules Seeman, Fred Zell, Barry Weiss, Karen Gamell, Marc and Judith Mann, Jack Trainham, Ken Stonebraker, Joan Madsen, John Lyons, Saul Neidorf, and M.R. Martin. Last, and most important, are the three most cherished women in my life. Sheryl, my partner of 40 years, is the Archangel—the Queen Bee—who has taught me so much and enhanced the quality of my life. My beautiful daughters, Kali Dawn and Leah Sunset, have brought me great pride and joy, and helped me find my purpose in life.

Introduction

This book was conceived and written in my head during 12 days in a hospital intensive care unit following an unexpected crisis of congestive heart failure at the age of 74. I was rushed to the hospital by ambulance and my condition was critical. I did not know if I would leave the hospital alive, considering that one of my brothers did die in a hospital from the very same genetic heart problem eight years earlier and at the same time of year. The low point was the day after I was hospitalized when my heart's "ejection fraction," or pumping power, was rated at 25 percent (normal is 50 percent to 65 percent), and a nurse asked me if I wanted to speak to the hospital chaplain. My brain heard that I was being offered last rites before dying. I was kept alive with five intravenous lines, including a Swanz-Ganz catheter through my neck into my heart and lungs. The medical trauma took place during the coronavirus pandemic when my family and friends could not visit. It was like a bad dream in which everyone who came into my hospital room—including nurses, phlebotomists, cardiologists, residents, and medical students—wore masks and face shields. Of course, it was not a dream and I was isolated and alone as I hovered in a precarious state between life and death. Lying in bed, deprived of my comfortable solar-powered home and meaningful work as a psychologist, I reviewed my life from birth to that present moment. Life review is what people tend to do when facing their mortality.

The medical crisis was not my first traumatic experience, only the most recent. I had been a victim of horrific and painful abuse as a child, and I had dealt with post-traumatic anxiety well into adulthood.

However, despite my painful childhood and other challenges, I have found a way to live a wonderful, fulfilling, and meaningful life. I have more than survived—I have thrived—and my trauma recovery has been full of blessings. I call these *triumphs*, and this book tells a true and personal story demonstrating that happiness is possible despite a trauma history.

This book is an account of my 74-year journey from traumas to triumphs that begins with 18 years in Hell's Kitchen, a violent, inner-city community in New York City. In Chapter 1, I reveal some of the painful and traumatic experiences of my childhood. In subsequent chapters, I share other traumatic experiences. But the goal of this book is to use my story to validate the possibility of a fulfilling life beyond recovery. My story details how I was able to discover my calling and enjoy a life with love, meaning, and purpose. Some of my triumphs involved what seemed like miracles or divine interventions. Some examples are receiving a full scholarship to Yale University; obtaining a PhD in clinical psychology in record time; writing four books on the topic of anxiety, including a publisher's best seller; a 20-year speaking business that took me all-expenses-paid to every state in the U.S. more than once, including several trips to Hawaii and Alaska, as well as international destinations in Cuba and all the Canadian provinces (with just one exception) from British Columbia to Nova Scotia. I have logged more than 500 international workshops and trainings over the 20-year period. Other highlights and successes include co-founding a Waldorf school, and creating a thriving psychology practice and therapist training center consisting of 17 therapists with a long waiting list for our services.

Virtually all forms of trauma, especially sexual and physical abuse, impact a victim's self-esteem, ability to trust, and sense of safety in the world. Victims may cope by disconnecting from their painful feelings, a defense known as *dissociation*, and those feelings may include shame, fear, vulnerability, distrust, and feeling "damaged." With young victims, innocence is prematurely lost and, in many cases, a secure childhood is never established. Anxiety is the most common outcome of trauma, with depression following closely, and the diagnosis of trauma- and stressor-related disorder, formerly called post-traumatic stress disorder (PTSD), is considered the most severe of all the anxiety disorders.

From my perspective, the ultimate goal of trauma recovery goes well beyond survival, which is why I do not think of myself as a survivor. True recovery means regaining the ability to trust, to love and be loved, to feel empowered and safe, to develop self-confidence, to be successful, to dream, to think optimistically, to discover one's purpose, and, if lucky, to live a fulfilling, meaningful life with happiness and purpose.

The prevalence of childhood trauma in the U.S. is staggering, and I am just one case example. In a 1998 large-scale, collaborative study by the Centers for Disease Control and Prevention and Kaiser Permanente Health Maintenance Organization in California, 17,421 adults were assessed for the prevalence of childhood adverse experiences (ACE). ACE includes sexual and physical abuse, emotional and physical neglect, impaired parents (addictions, mental illness), parental divorce, and household criminal activity. Sixty-seven percent of the sample group reported at least one ACE, and 22 percent reported three or more. Similar findings have been reported in other large-scale studies. For example, in 2011 the Substance Abuse and Mental Health Services Administration (SAMHSA) conducted a study of 14,733 children and found that 48 percent experienced loss of a caregiver, 47 percent witnessed domestic violence, and 44 percent were from families with an impaired caregiver. More recently, it has been recognized that childhood trauma can also include poverty, homelessness, abandonment, lack of comforting, unpredictability, witnessing violence of any kind, and narcissistic or immature parenting. This expanded definition of ACE has led to a new diagnosis: developmental trauma. I would be included in the high percent of victims who experienced multiple adverse childhood traumas.

Given the data on the prevalence of childhood trauma, we could reasonably conclude that we live in a culture that fosters trauma. Poverty, for example, is everywhere in our country, and 50 percent of children who live in poor, urban communities—a total of 74 million—will experience at least one trauma by age 18. Eighty-five percent will witness violence, and 66 percent will be directly injured. I am familiar with poverty-induced trauma, having grown up in a poor, inner-city community in New York City.

Rampant violence is also evident in media sources such as television, movies, and video games aimed at children. As an example, in a video game called *Grand Theft Auto Vice City*, a mobster just released from prison attempts to reestablish himself in the underworld as a cocaine dealer. Along the way, he gets involved in a gang war, runs a pornography studio, and commits assorted felonies, including bank robbery. Game players can pick up a prostitute and bring her into a dark alley. And violence in the game is brutal: You can beat anyone to death with an assortment of weapons. I witnessed enough violence in childhood to say that violence in the media imitates life, although there is also evidence that violence in the media can lead to real-life violence.

Topping *Vice City* in violence is another video game, *Postal 2*, by the game developer Running With Scissors. *Postal 2* is the sequel to the controversial *Postal*, which was banned in ten countries and whose makers were sued by the U.S. Postal Service. The new version was the first video game to earn an "M" (meaning for mature players, 17 and older) rating for "intense violence" from the Entertainment Software Rating Board. In *Postal 2* the goal is to kill or be killed, and its content includes decapitating police officers with shovels and slurs against gays and lesbians. Furthermore, the game shows Middle Eastern men perusing bomb-making and terrorism books at a library before opening fire with machine guns, and the lead character utters hateful and racist slurs while urinating and pouring gasoline on women and minorities before setting them on fire. The developer, of course, denies the game is linked to violent behavior. With an anticipated release date in 2021, Six Days in Fallujah is a new online shooting game that involves blatant violence using guns that look like real-life firearms for murdering opponents. The game maker, Epic, claims that it teaches history in that it is a simulation of the bloodiest battle during the Iraq War.

A national study of 1,178 children ages 8 to 18 found that almost 9 percent play video games more than 24 hours per week. Furthermore, 80 percent of 10-year-olds were found to own at least one gaming console that can access the web. It was also found that 25 percent of preschoolers use the internet regularly.

Violence is apparent in just the *names* of some video games: *Kill Zone, Resident Evil, God of War*, and *Call of Duty*, which was one of the best-selling games in the U.S. Violence is also evident in the names of some heavy metal rock bands, such as Napalm Death, Massacre, Severed Head in a Bag, Megadeath, and A Million Dead Cops.

The negative effect of violent video games is underscored by a report that the teenagers who shot fellow students at Columbine High School in Colorado in 1999 and shooters who have committed similar atrocities elsewhere were trained by common video games. It is also interesting to note that some branches of the military use commercially available video games for combat training and to desensitize soldiers to killing. Perhaps we should not be surprised when children or adolescents go out and kill after many hours of practicing murder simulations in video games.

Research on children's television programming has found significant violence on many shows and programs. Even Saturday morning cartoons include violence. One study found 47 violent acts per hour on Saturday morning cartoons, including hurting, maiming, and killing. Looking at the big picture, we see on a daily basis domestic terrorism, divisive politics, racially motivated hate crimes, and other forms of violence in our country.

Sexual abuse of children and adolescents is also systemic in the U.S., and probably globally. It occurs in churches, high school sports, Boy Scouts, and summer camps. My heart broke when I learned in 2016 that 368 preteen and teenage girls in the gymnastics world reported sexual abuse by coaches, gym owners, doctors, and other adults involved in the sport. In all, 115 adults in the gymnastics world were named, including highly regarded mentors, in every part of the U.S. Such child sexual abuse is probably underreported due to shame and fear, and the true numbers may never be known.

Sexual abuse of children is not limited to girls. By the age of maturity, as many as one in six boys in the U.S. has had unwanted sex with an adult or older child. The CDC-Kaiser study I mentioned earlier reported that 16 percent of males were sexually abused by age 18. Numerous studies have found similar results. A 1996 study of male university students in the Boston area reported that 18 percent of men were sexually abused before the age of 16, a percentage that is closer to one in five boys. Another national study reported that 16 percent of men were sexually abused by age 18. A 1998 study reviewing research on male childhood sexual abuse concluded that the problem is "common, underreported, underrecognized, and undertreated." Millions of men, abused as children, continue to live with the debilitating effects of trauma and broken trust. As a man who was assaulted and abused as a 13-year-old boy, I can be counted as a one-in-six victim.

The prevalence of the sexual abuse of boys is recognized by a support organization, 1in6.org. The organization was co-founded in 2007 by Greg Lemond, three-time winner of the Tour de France, in response to a lack of resources addressing the impact of negative childhood sexual experiences on the lives of adult men, one of many under-recognized aspects of childhood sexual abuse.

As I contemplated writing this book, I searched the literature for other books involving personal trauma recovery stories. I could find only one other published trauma recovery story written by a man. In his case, the primary trauma centered on mother-son sexual abuse. As mentioned earlier, at least five large-scale studies have found that 16 to 18 percent of men were sexually abused or assaulted before the age of 18. Few seek help and many suffer from the debilitating effects of trauma, which include post-traumatic stress disorder and other forms of anxiety, depression, substance abuse, suicidality, underachievement in school or at work, and problems in intimate relationships. I hope this book will help bring attention to the "one-in-six" statistic and encourage men, with support from their families, friends, and partners, to seek help.

While anxiety is a predictable response to childhood trauma, it is not the only long-term consequence. The ACE studies found a correlation between childhood adversity and health outcomes. High "doses" of ACEs increase the risk for heart disease, cancer, and chronic obstructive pulmonary disease" by 2.5 times the average. Four or more ACEs results in 4.5 times the average for depression, and 12 times the average for suicidality. It is entirely possible that my heart failure crisis was trauma-related, as was a respiratory crisis at age nine that resulted in a two-week hospitalization following an emergency tracheotomy in an ambulance.

Brain development is also compromised by childhood trauma. The prefrontal cortex—the brain area associated with critical thinking, executive functioning, and learning—is hijacked by an overactive base brain whose purpose is to keep us alive. As a result, trauma victims are more likely to exhibit poor judgment and engage in self-sabotage and high-risk behavior. The ACE studies suggest that the mechanism by which childhood trauma affects health involves the hypothalamic-pituitary axis—the body's stress response system. The long-term effects of trauma keep the stress response system in a chronic state of arousal that weakens the immune system.

Most children and adolescents suffering with the effects of trauma are not recognized and receive no help. Only an estimated 25 percent of trauma victims get professional help. In addition, there are gender differences in those who do find help. Women are three times more likely than men to seek therapy and, correspondingly, there are three times as many female therapists as there are male therapists. Men are less likely than women to seek help for the effects of trauma, largely due to cultural messages that boys and men should not be weak or need help. In contrast, girls and women are more socialized to talk about their feelings and they are more likely to seek professional help.

The term *recover* means to "regain," "recoup," or "retrieve" something that has been lost.

What is lost, or at least compromised, is the probability of actualizing one's innate potential. But the possibility of recovery always exists. My conviction that recovery from trauma is possible is based not only on my personal experience, but also on my observations during 47 years as a psychologist. I have witnessed many therapy clients transform their emotional pain into energy for actualizing their potential. They have moved on to experience a satisfying and meaningful life, find happiness and joy, and live fully with a sense of purpose. Some even become therapists who are uniquely equipped to resonate with the experience of trauma victims, and to inspire them to actualize their human potential.

Not all trauma victims achieve their potential, but that is also true for most people. One question I address in this book is, What is it that enables some people to overcome profound challenges and achieve happiness, joy, meaning, and purpose? In my case, part of the answer is that along the way, various people have come into my life to provide love, help, and support, often without even realizing their positive impact on me. I refer to them as "angels," and I have formulated what I call the "Angel Theory of Relationships." The idea is that during the course of a lifetime, we each have numerous relationships, some of which endure the test of time while others are short-lived or even end painfully. But if we grow or are enhanced in some way as a result of a relationship, or learn something important about ourselves, it could be said every relationship serves a *purpose*. While we do not consciously consider ourselves angels in each other's lives, it is likely that every relationship meets a need or serves a purpose. This way of looking at relationships has helped me, and many of my therapy clients over the years, to deal with trauma, heartbreak, and loss. We can be grateful for the personal growth or new learning that is attributable to each relationship. In this book, you will be introduced to some of the angels in my life and how they contributed to my triumph over trauma.

I also address the role of self-esteem in trauma recovery. In many cases of sexual abuse, including mine, victims tend to blame themselves. We may feel that we did not do enough to prevent or stop the abuse, or that in some way we attracted it or deserved it. Our self-esteem is compromised and we may avoid experiences that otherwise would be empowering, such as taking the chance to start a business, seeking a graduate degree, taking risks in relationships, and pursuing our dreams. On the other hand, I will discuss how trauma can lead to resilience and the discussion will include the key sources of high self-esteem.

Apart from the Angel Theory of Relationships, another source for resilience and recovery is the energy of anxiety itself. Anxiety manifests in various ways, such as worry, phobias, and panic attacks, but anxiety is also a source of energy. If that energy can be directed toward positive goals, it can be helpful in achieving self-actualization. For me, post-traumatic anxiety became the driving force that enabled me to thrive and achieve happiness. In this book, I will include suggestions for how to transform anxiety into motivation for doing the work required to live a satisfying life.

There are many approaches to successful trauma recovery, one of which involves learning self-regulation skills such as breath control. Fritz Perls, the psychiatrist who is credited with a recovery approach known as Gestalt therapy, suggested, "Anxiety is excitement without breath." We hold our breath when anxious, and if we train ourselves to breathe through anxiety, we can develop a sense of mastery and confidence that we can handle it. We know that the respiratory system regulates other organ systems, including cardiovascular and neuromuscular, and it is the one organ system we can voluntarily control. We also know that developing physical competence translates into emotional self-confidence. By developing control of our mind, body, and emotions, we can gain confidence in our ability to control other aspects of our lives. I have been blessed with opportunities to learn the skills that empowered me to achieve many of my life goals.

Trauma recovery does not necessarily require professional help. In fact, in one of my previous books, *Conquering Panic and Anxiety Disorders* (2002), I provide a commentary on 33 triumphant anxiety recovery cases, many of which did not involve therapy. The stories were elicited from a writers' website and my role in the project was to comment on each case, focusing on diagnoses and the steps taken to overcome the anxiety condition. Many were victims of abuse, and where therapy was not involved, there were other partners or angels who contributed to their successful anxiety recovery.

Techniques and strategies for trauma recovery will be ineffective for those who do not *believe* they can thrive. Recovery begins with how we think about what we experience. Being victimized does not mean we have to think of ourselves as victims. When we believe we can find a path to success, happiness, meaning, and fulfillment, we can transform the pain of trauma into motivation to achieve those goals. In this book I will refer to success, happiness, meaning, and fulfillment as *triumphs*.

These trauma recovery goals are idiosyncratic, meaning that people vary in their idea and experience of success, happiness, meaning and fulfillment. My idea of happiness aligns with a definition offered by the positive psychology researcher, Dr. Sonja Lyubomirsky, in her book *The How of Happiness* (2007). She describes happiness as "the experience of joy, contentment, or positive well-being, combined with a sense that one's life is good, meaningful, and worthwhile."

Based on the research of another positive psychologist, Dr. Martin Seligman, there are a host of self-tests for measuring personal happiness. These measures include the Authentic Happiness Inventory, General Happiness Scale, Satisfaction with Life Scale, Well-Being Survey, and Meaning in Life Questionnaire. These tests are free and available to the public, and they can be accessed at the Questionnaire Center of the University of Pennsylvania's Authentic Happiness web site: https://www.authentichappiness.sas.upenn.edu/testcenter.

The field of positive psychology has begun to focus on a phenomenon known as posttraumatic growth. The idea is that trauma and adversity provide opportunities for positive transformation in beliefs and behavior. Such positive changes include qualities of character such as generosity, love, purpose, and humility. My story is an example of the transformational relationship between trauma and the positive qualities that lead to happiness.

In addition to the personal challenges in trauma recovery, there are some significant cultural barriers to finding happiness and achieving one's potential. Each year starting in 2012, an independent World Happiness Report is published based on data from the Gallup World Poll and Llyod's Register Foundation. The report evaluates 156 countries on a happiness index and rank orders the countries surveyed. The criteria for determining a country's happiness index includes freedom to make personal life decisions, perception of corruption in government and business, healthy life expectancy at birth, generosity (monetary support for charities), purchasing power parity, prevalence of positive affect (laughter and enjoyment) and prevalence of negative affect (worry, sadness, and anger). In the 2019 World Happiness Report, the U.S. ranked 19th out of 156 countries. Finland was ranked highest in happiness, followed by Iceland, Denmark, Switzerland, The Netherlands, Sweden, Germany, and Norway. Also higher in happiness than the U.S. were New Zealand, Canada, Austria, Costa Rica, Israel, Luxemburg, Ireland, and Belgium. Based on these findings, it could reasonably be concluded that it is harder to be happy in the U.S. than in 18 other countries. In addition to our relatively low standing on measures of happiness, it was found that in the U.S., there are higher levels of anxiety, depression, addiction, and screen time (which the study suggests is inversely correlated with happiness).

Many people believe that more money makes you happier. A 2010 study conducted by Princeton University researchers found that more money does increase happiness with income up to about $75,000, at which point it tops out. This has led to the general belief that more money does not lead to greater happiness above the $75,000 threshold. However, a 2021 study at the Wharton Business School contradicts this belief. In the newer study, more than 33,000 employed participants used a phone app to provide in-the-moment snapshots of their feelings during daily life. The study found that all forms of well-being continued to rise with income with no inflection point where money stops to matter. In other words, more money does increase happiness. But there are some qualifications. The study also found that people who equate money with happiness are generally less happy. Furthermore, people who earned more money worked longer hours and felt more time, pressure, and stress. The study concluded that income is only a modest source of happiness.

Besides financial security, the other sources of happiness include strong social connections, meaningful work, creativity and a sense of purpose. In this book I discuss a community of people I met in Tennessee who referred to themselves as "voluntary peasants." They were a self-sufficient vegetarian community with a social structure that emphasized selflessness, ingenuity, and common purpose. They were spiritual but not religious in the conventional sense and seemed to be very happy.

This book is organized by the many places where I have lived from birth to age 74. Each location represents a period of my life, a stage of growth and maturation resulting from my experiences in each place. The relationships, schools, professional training, and jobs from each phase of my life have contributed to my successful journey from trauma to triumph. I feel that I have experienced a series of distinct lives associated with the many places I have lived and my experiences in those times and places. Some of these phases of my life seemed so intense and different from preceding periods that in retrospect they seem like a series of reincarnations. Like a butterfly emerging from caterpillar to a colorful flying insect, or a snake molting its skin while sliding into the next stage of development, I have experienced multiple reincarnations without actual bodily births and deaths.

My journey began in New York City, where I was born, followed in order by significant time periods in Montreal, New Haven, Miami, San Francisco, Nashville, Los Angeles/Santa Monica and several locations in Vermont. The amount of time spent in each location varies, yet psychologically each time period has been equally powerful and transformative. One year in San Francisco, for example, was as rich and impactful as three years in Nashville, or four years at Yale University in New Haven, or five years working as a psychologist in Southern California. On the other hand, my first 18 years growing up in Hell's Kitchen were the most poignant in terms of the traumas that haunted me for many years. Developmental psychology tells us that the earlier trauma or abuse occurs, the more likely it will leave deep emotional scars and long-lasting, deleterious effects.

CHAPTER 1

Hell's Kitchen

(1946–1968)

THE STORY OF A PERSON'S LIFE BEGINS, of course, with the parents. We are not delivered by a stork nor arrive with no family history or genetic makeup. A male sperm fertilizes a female egg and, if all goes well, an embryo becomes a fetus and after a long gestation period, an infant is born with the DNA and inherited characteristics of the two biological parents. Thereafter, nurture (early life experiences) interacts with nature (genetics) to form our personality and behavior patterns.

My mother, Doris Meier, was the second of two children born in Montreal, Quebec, to Anna Hammel, a German immigrant, and John Christopher Meier, an Austrian immigrant. The story is that the two met in England and traveled on the same boat to Canada. They had two children: Hilda and my mother, who was nine years younger. Growing up in Montreal, my mother went to public school and then to Concordia University, where she majored in biology and competed on the ski team.

My father, Arun Foxman, was also born in Montreal, of Russian immigrants. His father, Simcha Fuchsman, was an Orthodox Russian Jew who I understand was a plumber by trade. Unfortunately, his mother, Anna Hirshbein, took her own life when Arun was a 12-year-old boy. I believe he was the first to discover her body in the backyard, and so trauma runs deep in the family tree.

Arun was the third of three children. The oldest was Faye, followed by Nathan. Arun's father broke Jewish tradition by remarrying in less than one year to Bryna, and the couple had three more children: Edith, Hyman, and Julius. I have fond memories of holiday visits with Aunt Faye and Uncle Harry, who lived in the Bronx, as well as several touching visits in Montreal with Edith before she died. Before meeting my mother, Arun married Amelia Romano, but the marriage was short-lived and no children were born.

Whereas my mother went to college, my father was saddled with responsibility for financially supporting his family beginning in high school. Thus, he did not have an opportunity to go to college. This was unfortunate because he was an intellectual man who loved theater and the arts. He was embittered by his family responsibility but, on the other hand, my father's high value on education as a ticket to success was instilled in me at an early age.

My parents apparently met on a public bus in Montreal. My mother was reading a newspaper and my father was leaning over to read the news as well. As they looked up at each other, a spark was ignited and a relationship ensued. After they married, my parents emigrated to New York City, which was, and still is, the epicenter of live theater. They landed in Canarsie, a residential section of Brooklyn named after its first settlers, the Canarsie Indians. My father dove into the theater as a play director, but he also had another agenda. He wanted to join the United States Army in order to "fight Hitler," as he phrased it.

Ironically, my father was a pacifist who would not carry a weapon. He signed up as a medic and trained with the 10th Mountain Division in Colorado. The unit was an Army ski squadron, preparing to enter the war via helicopters in the Italian Alps.

I was, and still am as I write this life story, a baby boomer. We are a wave of births following World War II when returning soldiers started families and raised children. We number some 76 million children born between 1945 and 1964.

On my father's return from the war, my parents moved into a city-subsidized housing project known as the Amsterdam Houses on the West Side of Manhattan. The "projects," as they were called, consisted of numerous 6-story and 13-story brick apartment buildings extending from 61st Street to 64th Street, between Amsterdam Avenue and West End Avenue. I spent my first 18 years at 63 Amsterdam Avenue, apartment 6E.

Amsterdam Avenue, also known as 10th Avenue, was a truck route through Manhattan, a dividing line to be crossed to access the rest of the city. It was a fitting location for walking to the Actors Studio and the Theater District of New York City, where my father wanted to work. On the other hand, living along a truck route made it almost impossible to block out the vibration, lights, and diesel engine noise of trucks rolling through constantly. It was difficult to sleep at night.

Unfortunately, there were two even more significant problems with the Amsterdam Houses. First, as the white middle class were able to move out of the city to the suburbs of New York, the housing project became increasingly a ghetto for the less fortunate. The area became a predominantly Puerto Rican and Black community with many broken families. The bakeries, meat and fish markets, and fruit and vegetable vendors on Amsterdam Avenue all slowly disappeared. My parents' divorce when I was 10 years old set us back financially. It is common for a family's standard of living to decline following a divorce, and for an emotional toll to result from the breakup. In my case, I was unable to escape the trauma of growing up in what became a poor, violent, unsafe, inner-city, multiethnic community.

The second problem with the Amsterdam Houses was that they were located adjacent to Hell's Kitchen, a neighborhood on the West

Side of Manhattan bordered—according to historians—by 41st Street on the south, 59th Street on the north, 8th Avenue to the east, and the Hudson River to the west. I would include the Amsterdam Houses up to 66th Street, and I could make a strong case for Hell's Kitchen to extend up to 72nd Street. I lived in Hell's Kitchen from 1946 to 1964, well before the gentrification of the West Side that started in the 1990s, when development pressures began driving people of modest means to leave and when co-op apartments replaced the slum housing.

There was one particularly seedy housing section, known as the Phipps Houses, encircled by the Amsterdam projects. Originally constructed in 1910 by philanthropist Henry Phipps Jr., the houses were the first affordable housing units in the U.S. Designed at the time as quality housing for people of color, by the time I grew up, the neighborhood had been declared a "slum" by the New York City mayor's office. Jazz legend Thelonious Monk grew up in the Phipps Houses. I remember the Phipps Houses as dark apartments where prostitutes, pimps, and drug addicts hung out. There was also a jazz bar, named "the Jungle" by locals, a few blocks north of the Amsterdam Houses. I am certain it was also the site of a drug trade, and I remember shiny Cadillacs and limousines stopping by with well-dressed Black folks along with body guards making a visit. Some of them are likely to have been other famous jazz musicians and the vibe was one of secrecy.

In addition, the neighborhood included several east-west streets, from 61st to 66th, between Amsterdam and 9th Avenues. On these streets were slum apartment houses that were eventually torn down when the Lincoln Center for the Performing Arts began construction in 1959. Lincoln Center became a 16.3-acre complex of buildings, consisting of 30 indoor and outdoor facilities that host 5 million visitors annually. It opened its doors in 1962 and is now a vital part of

New York City's cultural hub. Included in the complex are the New York City Ballet, the Metropolitan Opera House, and the New York Philharmonic. I could never have imagined that the poor, violent, and traumatic neighborhood in which I grew up would be completely transformed into high culture.

Even after Lincoln Center opened its doors, the surrounding neighborhood was unsafe. I remember, for example, going to a show at Lincoln Center when I was in college.

When I parked my car on a side street, I left my guitar in its case on the back seat floor as it would not fit in the trunk of my small Fiat 650. While I was inside, the car was burglarized and the guitar was stolen. That is typical of New York City, where one could turn the corner from one neighborhood and enter an entirely different community. When I reported the guitar theft to the police, they literally laughed at me and said, "What do you want us to do about it?"

Until the 1970s, Hell's Kitchen was a bastion of poor and working-class immigrants, including Irish Americans, Italian Americans, and Greek Americans. Its reputation was gritty, but it was truly an ethnic melting pot. One of the few blessings growing up in this area was my exposure to people of all colors, cultures, and nationalities. I attended public schools throughout Hell's Kitchen, including kindergarten through fifth grade at P.S. 51 on 44th Street, and sixth through eighth grade at P.S. 191 on 59th Street. I remember walking home from school on Amsterdam Avenue. As I passed a bar on 47th Street, I noticed two police officers being given an envelope by the bartender. The officers looked around furtively as if to ensure they were not seen accepting the envelope. Even though I was young, probably 11 years old, I knew I had just witnessed corruption and grift.

My high school, located on 66th Street between Eighth and Ninth avenues, was called the High School of Commerce. Within the large school was the Horace Mann School, a program designed to accommodate the more promising and motivated students. Nevertheless, the future was bleak for most of my friends and acquaintances. Few were college-bound and some used the military as a ticket out of Hell's Kitchen. A high school student could sign up for the Army, Navy, Merchant Marines, or Air Force and, if accepted, have a chance at a trade education, a basic income along with room and board, and a uniform to wear proudly during visits to the home community. There were no wars on the horizon so it seemed safe to enlist. I, however, planned to go to college. But I remember distinctly the school guidance counselor laughing disdainfully at me when I told her I was planning to apply to Yale University. "There is no way you will be accepted," she chided. One of my fondest memories was the day I showed her my acceptance letter that included a full scholarship. My admittance to Yale is a story in itself, to be told in Chapter 3.

My first traumatic experience was an emergency tracheotomy that began in an ambulance when I was nine years old. I had the croup, a respiratory infection that makes it difficult to breathe, particularly at night. My brain woke me up when my oxygen level declined due to a phlegm obstruction in my windpipe. I tried to call for help but couldn't make a sound. I remember banging on the wall of the bedroom I shared with my younger brother, Marc, and then I fell unconscious. There was no 911 system in place in 1954, but a call to my doctor got him to rush to our apartment. Dr. Tannenbaum called an ambulance, got in, and performed the tracheotomy using a pocket knife and fountain pen cap to open up my airway. I woke up in the hospital the next day in five-point restraints, employed to keep me still and prevent me from pulling out the tube from the ventilator to my throat. I spent the next two weeks in the hospital recovering from the medical trauma and undergoing the psychological trauma of a near-death experience.

The next traumatic experience was my parents' divorce a year later when I was 10. I was aware of the tension and conflict between my parents, so it was not a complete surprise when they broke up. Nevertheless, to see my father leave us—three young children and my mother—was devastating. What was worse is that my parents continued to fight for another 10 years while I was growing up. Furthermore, as is the case with many divorces, our standard of living went down and I grew up in relative poverty, acutely aware of social class differences.

The best and most comprehensive study ever done on the effect of divorce on children began in 1970. Psychologists Judith Wallerstein, Joan Kelly, and some colleagues followed 131 children of divorce for 25 years. They published several books about their findings: *Surviving the Breakup* (1980), *Second Chances: Men, Women and Children, a Decade After Divorce* (1989), *The Unexpected Legacy of Divorce* (2000), and *What About the Kids: Raising Children Before, During, and After Divorce* (2003). The primary finding contradicted previous theories about divorce when they concluded that the impact of divorce on children manifests in adulthood when they begin to deal with relationship issues, such as commitment and whether or not to have children. Furthermore, the researchers found that the impact of divorce on children is determined not so much by the acute breakup, but more by the ongoing, post-divorce, co-parenting relationship that can last for years.

Wallerstein identified four types of co-parenting styles after divorce, and it should be obvious which of them are most likely to have negative effects—such as anxiety and low self-esteem—on the children. The four co-parenting styles are:

1. Perfect Pals: These are co-parents who share decision-making and child-rearing responsibilities. They respect each other and are capable of doing family activities together. They may even maintain their friendship with each other.

2. Cooperative Colleagues: While not friends with each other, these co-parents can work together for the sake of their children. They communicate amicably, share parenting responsibilities, and control their feelings and underlying conflicts.

3. Angry Associates: Adversarial battles and ongoing anger are characteristics of these co-parents after divorce. In this type of relationship, there are frequent conflicts around custody and visitations.

4. Fiery Foes: In this hostile relationship, the ex-spouses have no capacity for cooperation as parents. They are the parents whose battles return to court because they are unable to communicate with each other.

The post-divorce, co-parent relationship between my parents would fit the Angry Associate category, if not Fiery Foes. They fought frequently and, unfortunately, they put me in the middle of their conflicts. They used me as a messenger since they were unable to communicate amicably. It was an extremely uncomfortable and anxiety-arousing position. Naturally, parents who cannot get along while married are likely to have difficulty cooperating after divorce. But the level of hostility between my parents was extreme. I recall, for example, their argument on the street after my high school graduation. They could not agree on which restaurant we would visit to celebrate my high school success and admission to Yale. I think the underlying issue was about the cost of dinner out.

When I was 10, my mother took me to see a therapist at the Jewish Family Service in Manhattan. I remember my mother telling me on the subway, "Pay attention to which train we are taking and the stop where we will be getting off, because after today you will be going by yourself." The "presenting problem" for which I was to get help was my feeling guilty, angry, and sad about my father leaving the family, an all-too-common reaction in children when their parents break up.

The counseling service was on an upper floor of a tall office building that required an elevator to reach. On the street level was a soda shop, a chrome and vinyl diner-style restaurant specializing in milkshakes and ice cream sodas. I recall vividly a specific therapy session in which the therapist invited me down to the soda shop and said, "Feel free to order anything you want." I ordered a chocolate milkshake, which was delivered in the tallest glass I had ever seen. After I finished drinking the thick and delicious milkshake, he asked me a question I will never forget as long as I live: "Would you like to have another one?" I must have turned red with guilt because I did want a second milkshake, which I must have thought was more than I deserved. Through this metaphor, the therapist was helping me address my guilt about the family breakup, and I got the message: "It's not your fault, and it's OK to want more than you have." The second chocolate milkshake was as delicious as the first.

Fear haunted me throughout my childhood in Hell's Kitchen, in great part due to the violence I witnessed in this volatile community. The Broadway play *West Side Story* portrays the tension and violence I experienced in this primarily Puerto Rican and Black community. Some sharp images and memories stand out about this aspect of my childhood. Racial tension was high, and, as a White boy, I was an accessible target for racial hostility. When I dated a Puerto Rican girl, for example, I was threatened and physically harassed by a group of Puerto Rican boys who said, "We don't want you messing around with our women." I did have a Puerto Rican girlfriend in middle school, Yvette, but we had to fly under the radar to avoid vengeful punishment by the Puerto Rican boys.

Many other forms of violence surrounded me in Hell's Kitchen. I recall a hunting knife being thrown into the lobby of my apartment building, entering blade first into the elevator wall near me. While bicycling in Central Park, my brother, Marc, was mugged and had his bicycle stolen. An aggressive boy pushed another from a pier to his death in the Hudson River. A friend of mine, who I can still vividly picture, was beaten regularly by a brutal father. He finally ran away from home, and I never saw him again. Although I never witnessed it, there were reports of violent gangs from "uptown," with names like the Viceroys and the Marlboros, who would fight with pipes and chains. These violent occurrences and images certainly contributed to my unease and anxiety.

I was myself a victim of sexual assault. On the way to middle school at age 12, I naively agreed to help an adult Black man remove a piece of furniture from one of the abandoned buildings on 63rd Street. As I stepped inside, he grabbed me in a headlock and pulled me to the back of the building. I recall vividly the sound of broken glass and rubble as my feet dragged along the floor. He then threatened to "smash my head" with the brick he held over me if I did not do what he said or if I ever told anyone. He then raped me in the most violent and humiliating way. I felt certain he would kill me and leave me among the broken bricks, glass, and rubble. I considered trying to run for my life, but I could not take the chance. Besides, I could not run with my pants down. I was so frightened that I not only complied, but due to feeling so ashamed, I was unable to tell anyone about the painful trauma for more than 10 years. I was always on the lookout for that man and, unbelievably, I did see him on one occasion roaming the neighborhood. There must have been other victims. Of all the traumatic experiences I suffered, this was the most horrifying and devastating.

There were some other loathsome instances of sexual abuse that I am still uncomfortable revealing in public. Suffice it to say that all the abuse situations were perpetrated by adult men. Therefore, I can identify with women who have been sexualized, objectified, exploited, or abused by men. I recall, for example, being stalked by a man with an unsavory look in his eyes. I escaped by entering a large, crowded department store and winding my way out of another entrance. Being stalked and abused may have been the result of my physical appearance: I once overheard some Puerto Rican girls in high school refer to me as "¡Que lindo!" which in Spanish means, "How cute!" or "How good-looking!" or, "Isn't he hot?!"

I believe my interest in joining the track team in school stemmed from the trauma experiences, especially those where I felt trapped. I qualified for the track team in junior high, and I eventually became the high school's team captain. My event was the 440-yard dash, or quarter mile, now known as the 400 meters. This was a distance at which one could not run all out. It was a tactical race that required speed combined with patience, while saving a kick for the final stretch. My distance was also one leg on the mile relay (4x440 yards), and I often competed in the two events at the same track meet. I medaled frequently, clocking times hovering at 48 seconds for the quarter mile, and I had the dubious reputation as the "fastest white boy in New York City." Almost all the high school teams we competed against, including Brooklyn Boys High School and a host of others, consisted primarily of Black track and field athletes. For some reason, the long-distance events favored white runners and the sprints favored Black runners. I was not the overall fastest runner in New York City and my medal collection consists of silver and bronze, although I did win a gold medal at one meet. I gave that medal to my high school girlfriend on a chain to wear as a necklace.

Racial violence was ever-present throughout my years in Hell's Kitchen, even on the track team in high school. For example, a Black member of the track team punched me in the face in the locker room while mouthing a racial slur. His name was Laverne, and apparently he believed I was flirting with his girlfriend. I was certainly popular in high school but I can assure you that I was not flirting with Laverne's girlfriend. Keep in mind I was one of only two white athletes on the team, the other being Paul, a smart, Italian American long-distance runner who kept to himself. Being a white boy serving as team captain may not have sat well with some of the Black athletes.

Every year a college track meet, known as the Penn Relays, takes place in Philadelphia at the University of Pennsylvania track and field facility. The college meet includes one high school relay event and, based on our record in New York City, my team qualified for the event. I recall vividly our track coach giving us each a note on the train to Philadelphia: "Dress like gentlemen, act like gentlemen, and run like animals!" The Penn Relays is an exhibition event, where college track coaches come to identify high school talent. We performed well and the Olympic track coach, Bob Giegengack, who led the U.S. track team in the 1964 Olympics, spotted me and encouraged me to apply to Yale. Giegengack was also the Yale University track coach. I did apply and was accepted with a full scholarship. Tuition, room, and board at Yale for 2019–20 is $55,000 per year. In 1964 when I was accepted, the full cost was $3,000 per year, still more than my family could afford.

As I mentioned earlier in this chapter, I have generally been uncomfortable with men due to my trauma history. In addition, since I grew up with my mother and no father in the home, I was much more comfortable and familiar with women. Nevertheless, over the years I developed some significant and positive relationships with men who served as mentors. The first such relationship was with my high school track coach, Marty Spielman. On the surface, "Mr. Spielman," as we called him, was a serious man who walked quickly and spoke sharply. The team knew he meant business. I sensed he knew my story and he stepped in as a father figure, encouraging me not only as an athlete but also as a person. He recognized my potential, considering that I was a good student with leadership qualities evident in my role as editor of the school yearbook and captain of the track team. My father did not attend even one of my track and field meets to see me compete during high school, but Mr. Spielman was always there cheering me on. I owe a debt of gratitude to Mr. Spielman for the opportunities that resulted in my successful application to Yale.

I can introduce some other men who supported me at various stages of life. Jules Seeman, PhD, was my adviser in the doctoral program in clinical psychology at Vanderbilt University in Nashville, Tennessee. Remarkably, while most doctoral students experience anxiety about completing their PhD research and passing their oral examinations, Jules said to me at the end of my first year in the program, "Paul, you have proven yourself worthy of the PhD. Our task now is simply for you to do the work and complete the program." Jules also shaved a year off the usual five-year PhD program by suggesting that I assemble a committee of psychology professors to examine me on a study I coauthored and published in a prestigious journal as a senior at Yale. His idea was that if I could demonstrate the skills and knowledge of empirical research equivalent to a master's thesis, I could get credit for the master's thesis requirement. The idea worked, and in four years, I may have earned the fastest PhD ever awarded in a clinical psychology program approved by the American Psychological Association.

Let me also introduce Saul Neidorf, a psychiatrist who was my training analyst during my predoctoral internship at Mount Zion Hospital and Medical Center in San Francisco, California. We remained friends after I returned to graduate school. I once visited him in Freeport, Maine, when he took a job as director of a residential treatment center for children, and he visited me in Vermont after I had my first child. Saul had a profound influence on my therapeutic style as a practicing psychologist. He is always in the room with me.

I could also mention David Fassler, a psychiatrist who invited me to start the Vermont Center for Anxiety Care, in a historic building he owned in Burlington. In 1999, the year my mother died, I relocated to this picturesque waterfront location on Lake Champlain. Some people have said we have the nicest offices in all of Vermont. I created what has become a thriving, premier practice with 17 therapists receiving supervision from me toward their licenses in psychology, clinical social work, mental health counseling, and marriage and family therapy. David and I have had our business conflicts, but we have been partners in this successful enterprise for more than two decades. I recently met with David to discuss my ideas for a succession plan. In light of my medical crisis, I told him that I was thinking of replacing myself with a psychologist who had the right combination of skills: eligibility to supervise the staff toward licensure, a "rainmaker" who could attract new business, effective leadership qualities, and an interest in running a business. David's response was, "I never met anyone like you. Your staff are there because of you, and if you leave, many of them would also leave. I trust your clinical and administrative judgment. It will be very difficult to find a replacement. I hope you stay as long as possible."

Marc Mann, PhD, was another professional influence. Although we are roughly the same age, I viewed him as an older brother who had business experience from his family history whereas I had none. I met Marc when I was conducting a site visit for one of my students while teaching in the master's psychology program at Antioch New England Graduate School in Keene, New Hampshire. Marc and his wife, Judith, owned a psychology practice located in Essex Junction, Vermont, and we connected during the site visit. Within months, I joined their practice, named Family Therapy Associates, bringing with me my expertise in child therapy and clinical supervision of interns. One of my titles was Director of Training and we added some interns to the staff, which grew to 18 therapists and two secretaries. We became partners in the business, built a 6,000-square-foot office building funded by a Small Business Administration loan using our homes as equity, and we worked together for some 15 years. We had our business conflicts but I learned a lot from Marc about running a business. When we dissolved the partnership, I started my own corporation, Paul Foxman, PhD, Inc., and I went on to create the Vermont Center for Anxiety Care. Ironically, after our "business divorce," Marc told me he respected and looked up to me. I had no clue that he felt that way about me. We reconciled and we are friends to this day.

In addition to these professional relationships, I have some other friends whom I trust and with whom I feel a special kindship. One is Karen, who I met in Florida at a residential treatment center in Miami. Karen was a house parent and I was the residential supervisor. I have known Karen longer than anyone else, and we remain friends to this day.

More recently, I met Fred in Vermont. Thanks to our many common interests, we connected quickly. We both enjoy riding our motorcycles, playing guitar, and having spiritual discussions that we refer to a "sanghas." We also share an affinity for using marijuana as a sacrament and to enhance our weekly music sessions. We are like brothers and spend as much time together as possible. We once did an 1,800-mile round-trip motorcycle journey, riding in formation, to a BMW motorcycle rally in Lima, Ohio. We stopped in Pittsburgh on the way, where Fred grew up and where I met his widowed father. We also spent some time at an empty camp where his family spent many summers, and where we swam in the pond to refresh ourselves on the return trip to Vermont. Knowing that my children live in Boston, Fred once said of his brotherhood with me, "If you ever move to Boston, I will die."

Despite the rocky relationship with my father, which included long periods with no contact, I credit him for several positive influences. First was his intelligence and emphasis on education. While he was unable to help me financially with educational expenses, he was proud of my academic achievements. Another blessing was that he introduced me to the guitar, which I started playing as a child. He was an aspiring performing artist who took guitar and voice lessons, and I tagged along when his guitar teacher came to our apartment once a week to give lessons. I played guitar on and off over the years, but stopped altogether in graduate school when it was clear that a choice was necessary. Due to time constraints, I had to choose between being a musician and a psychologist. I could not do both during the rigorous PhD program.

I knew in my heart that I would someday start to play guitar again. In 2012, after a hiatus of more than 30 years, I purchased a beautiful, new, custom-made Martin electric-acoustic guitar, and I have been playing virtually every day and writing songs since then. My guitar was hand-selected at Martin Guitars' custom shop in the Nazareth, Pennsylvania, facility by Jeff Wheel, an owner of the local music store in Burlington, Vermont. I would classify my genre as singer-songwriter. I give thanks to my father for guitar and music, and I have one of his old guitars hanging as a decoration on a wall in my home office.

My father also introduced me to live theater in New York City. Due to the cost of theater tickets, we did not go often. But when we did, it was always magical. I saw *Hair*, *Joseph and the Amazing Technicolor Dreamcoat Coat*, and *Fiddler on the Roof*, as well as music performances at Carnegie Hall. As a result, I developed an interest in becoming a Broadway dancer, an interest that stayed with me well into adulthood. Whenever I am in New York, typically to teach workshops for mental health professionals, I always take in a Broadway play. I also look for opportunities to attend theater and music events wherever I live and travel.

Finally, my father was a pacifist who had a strong moral objection to war and killing. He would not permit me to own even a water gun, which was a popular toy in Hell's Kitchen. I remember asking for a Daisy Air Rifle as a Christmas/Hanukkah present. This was a toy gun that shot a cork attached to a string after cocking the mechanism. One had to push the cork back into the barrel for each shot. My father did not approve, but my mother prevailed. My father's pacifism influenced me and contributed to my successful application to become a conscientious objector during the Vietnam War. The conscientious objector classification required me to serve for two years in a "nonmilitary capacity in the national interest." I will describe my alternative service in Chapters 5 and 6.

After my parents divorced, and while I lived with my mother and brothers in the Amsterdam Houses, my mother went to Hunter

College in New York City to obtain a master's degree in psychology. She interned at Roosevelt Hospital (now Mount Sinai West) and went to work as a school psychologist for the Bureau of Child Guidance, a department within the New York public school system. She worked for 37 years as a school psychologist. One of my responsibilities was to start dinner each night so we could all eat together when my mother came home. I thank her for teaching me to cook, a set of skills I continued to develop and a hobby I enjoy to this day. I also admire my mother for the determination and commitment it took to go to graduate school while raising three boys.

I met Debbie at the High School of Commerce and we became sweethearts, spending hours on the phone each evening. She was about five feet, two inches tall with big blue-green eyes and shiny, long brown hair down to her waist. Debbie lived with her parents in Greenwich Village, within walking distance of Washington Square, known as the heart of an outdoor New York folk music scene. On any day of the week, one could hang out on Washington Square and listen to live folk music.

Debbie was clearly from a higher social class. Her parents had three apartments on the same floor of a building at 110 East 10th Street: one for the parents, one for Debbie and her older brother, and one for the family cook. Around the corner were some upscale food stores and delicatessens. Fifty years later, in 2021, the rent for just *one* apartment in the four-story building ranged from $11,500 to $16,000 *per month*.

To my mother's dismay, Debbie's parents took me in as a member of their family. They saw me as a good catch for their daughter and I, in turn, found an intact family that met my unmet need for belonging to a family. Once I was at Yale, I took the train almost every weekend from New Haven to New York City to spend time with Debbie in her apartment. I did not tell my mother about these visits as I knew she would not approve. Debbie's brother was rarely there and we had the apartment to ourselves. In the mornings, Debbie's mother would bring fresh-squeezed orange juice to us in bed, which I thought was both weird and wonderful.

Unfortunately, there was a blatant expectation on the part of Debbie's parents that in exchange for being so well taken care of, I would marry their daughter. There was pressure for us to marry even before I completed college. On one occasion, while Debbie and her mother were out shopping, they "found the perfect engagement ring" and arranged for her father to lend me the $500 to buy it ($500 in 1967 would be equivalent to $3,900 in 2021, as I write this book). I was in New Haven at the time and I did not even see the ring until after this arrangement was made. I remember walking down the aisle at the Marie Antoinette Ballroom at the One Fifth Avenue Hotel to my own wedding, thinking to myself, *I don't want to do this. How do I get out?* We were married while I was a junior at Yale, but it was just four months after the wedding when I had the courage to speak up and leave. We were able to have the marriage annulled, and as far as I know there is no official record of the marriage. Debbie was dramatic, and I'll never forget her lying on the apartment floor—the very floor I personally sanded and refinished along with painting the apartment in pink and orange—accusing me of murder. Breaking up was intensely painful for both of us, as it usually is for most couples.

While I was an undergraduate, my mother moved to an apartment building known as Riverview Towers in the area known as Harlem. This was a step up from the Amsterdam Houses, but it was still an inner-city location with its share of danger. The building was surrounded by old apartment houses and Puerto Rican supermarkets. At one point, a bullet went through a bedroom window in my mother's apartment at an angle suggesting it was fired from street level up to the 19th floor.

My mother had a friend, Eleanor, who was a psychologist with the U.S. Army. They met as members of the New York Psychological Association, where my mother was the organization's treasurer. Eleanor never married and had no family, and she willed her estate to my mother before she died. This enabled my mother to purchase with cash a co-op apartment at Lincoln Towers, just a few blocks from the Amsterdam Houses where I grew up. This turned out to be a wise investment as the property value skyrocketed over the years. In her Last Will and Testament, my mother bequeathed the sale value of the apartment in equal shares to her three sons, which gave each of us a financial boost. She also gave a financial gift to her three grandchildren: my two daughters and my brother Eric's son, Daniel. I invested part of the inheritance as a startup fund for my psychology practice, and put the rest in the bank for a measure of financial security. Only in retrospect can I appreciate how hard my mother worked to fulfill her commitment as a single parent. All I knew for many years was that I was on my own, with little parental support and guidance. In effect, I raised myself.

CHAPTER 2

Sainte-Agathe-Des-Monts, Quebec

(1946–1964)

I THINK OF MY MATERNAL GRANDFATHER, John Christopher Meier, as the spiritual figure in the family tree. He was a tailor in Montreal by trade, but he had the foresight to purchase 150 acres of land in the Laurentian Mountains, 70 miles north of the city. On the land was a rustic cottage with no plumbing or electricity at the time of purchase, and the property included a sizable lake where I learned to swim, fish, and kayak. The lake is on the map as Lac Beauchamp, which translates to English as "Lake of the Beautiful Fields." The property was nine miles out from a popular summer resort town, Sainte-Agathe, with an even larger lake frequented by power boats with water skiers and kiteboarders. I am certain my grandfather had in mind that this cottage would be a restorative summer home for his two daughters and their children.

Indeed, I spent 18 consecutive summers at Lac Beauchamp, in stark contrast to the concrete jungle of Hell's Kitchen. I believe the Laurentian Mountains saved my soul from a traumatic childhood and adolescence. My mother, who worked as a school psychologist, had the summers off and each Labor Day, as we took the train from Montreal back to New York City, her heart sank and her depression was palpable. I, too, felt like returning to New York City was going into a dark and dismal place, whereas in the mountains, I felt like I was "out." *Out* meant being outdoors, experiencing the healing power of nature.

The Lac Beauchamp cottage was modest, with two bedrooms downstairs, a kitchen with a wood stove, an open dining room/living room, and eventually an indoor bathroom. Before the plumbing was installed, we used on outhouse and bathed in galvanized tubs with creek water warmed in kettles on the wood stove. The first-floor walls were covered with knotty pine tongue and groove boards, which I thought was absolutely amazing, bringing nature inside. A staircase led to an open second floor curtained off into separate bedrooms for the children. In addition, there were two finished bedrooms upstairs, one used by my grandfather after my grandmother died, and the other by my Aunt Hilda and Uncle Alphonse. There was a pot-belly, wood-burning Buck Stove in the living room on the first floor, which was lit every morning to take the chill from the house even in July and August. The ashes from the wood stove were used to sprinkle into the outhouse hole, which served as a toilet. I learned about recycling and zero waste as a young child at Lac Beauchamp.

"Pa," as we called my grandfather, was a naturalist in the tradition of John Muir and Henry David Thoreau. Thoreau wrote the book *Walden*, a reflection on simple living in natural surroundings. Walden Pond is a real pond located in Concord, Massachusetts, where Thoreau lived in a cabin. Pa taught me how to pick mushrooms and wild blueberries, how to repair things with spruce gum direct from the trees, and how to fly-fish for the rainbow trout that were plentiful in the lake. Pa also had a prolific garden with carrots, peas, string beans, lettuce, broccoli, and other vegetables, which we picked and enjoyed at dinner. I sometimes picked a carrot, washed it off in the creek, and ate it on the spot. Those were the most flavorful carrots I have ever tasted, and as an adult, I make carrot juice using large, organic carrots reminiscent of Pa's garden. In addition, there was an apple tree on the property with tart but flavorful apples. As a child at Lac Beauchamp, I learned about self-sufficiency and "making do with what you have."

Before sunrise, Pa was on the lake, paddling and fly-fishing from a handmade kayak. Of course, he tied his own flies and had an amazing collection of colorful lifelike bait flies. He also had a birch bark canoe that he kept up with spruce gum when it sprang a leak. That canoe so represented our summer salvation that my brother, Marc, actually brought the canoe to New York City to hang in his basement apartment as a souvenir after our grandparents died and the property was sold.

I had a summer friend, Daniel, who lived year-round with his mother and sister a mile down the gravel road from our Lac Beauchamp cottage. I believe his father died when he was younger, and the family was dirt poor. Daniel was my age and spoke only French, but we communicated with a mixture of my broken French, his broken English, and unofficial sign language. We spent hours playing together during the summers. We would portage through the woods with the canoe held above our heads seeking ponds full of lily pads on which to explore. We walked barefoot all summer even on the gravel road separating our homes. We once made stilts from a scrap of two-by-four lumber and we could walk the entire mile with them. Daniel had access to a .22 rifle and introduced me to target practice using tin cans as targets. I also had a bow and arrow set that I used with targets mounted on straw bales. We fancied ourselves to be Indians and we developed many wilderness survival skills.

Each summer on our way to Lac Beauchamp, we would stop to visit an elderly woman known as Madame Lesaux. She spoke only French and during the visit, she would always read the lines in my mother's palms as well as the tea leaves left at the bottom of her teacup. Her readings would be translated to English by her adult

daughter with whom she lived. As she did the readings, Madame
Lesaux looked deeply into my mother's eyes, as though she were gathering telltale information. I sensed they all knew this was a guessing
game while pretending to be a serious matter of mediumship. When
the visit ended, my mother would unobtrusively give her some money
for her services.

Each evening, after dinner and kitchen cleanup, my mother and
my brothers, along with her sister, Hilda, and Hilda's daughters, would
go for a walk, snacking along the way on candy or chocolate. My
favorite confection was the Cadbury fruit and nut chocolate bar. We
gave names to the natural features along the gravel road: "Slanting
Rock Pool," "Birch Road," and the "Sand Dunes." The air temperature
dropped significantly when the sun set and we each took an old plaid
flannel shirt from an amazing collection hanging on hooks near the
door. These shirts were probably hand-me-down garments, and they
had the smoky smell of the wood-burning stove. After our walks, we
played board games at the dining room table illuminated by kerosene
lamps. After all, there was no radio, television, or other form of entertainment. The games I recall playing included Scrabble, Monopoly,
Chutes and Ladders, Parcheesi, and a variety of card games.

When I was 14 years old, I took a summer job as a counselor-in-
training at Camp Lewis, a refuge for inner-city boys from Montreal.
The camp was located on a chain of lakes some 10 miles from Lac
Beauchamp. I was invited back for three more summers, during which
I moved up in responsibility to cabin director (eight boys in a cabin),
and then to tribe director, responsible for three cabins. I will never
forget another tribe director, Andy, who played the banjo. I can still
hear that unmistakable banjo sound.

I became close friends with yet another tribe director, a Greek fellow named Elias. On our afternoons off, we would canoe out through

a chain of lakes so vast that it was easy to get lost and have trouble navigating back to camp. But there was one stop we always made. It was a small island with high, rocky cliffs. After testing the depth of the water below the towering rock ledges, we would dive off the ledges into the water below. We were careful to dive out far enough to clear the protruding ledges below. We carried a small can of white paint and each time we visited, we painted a line to mark the height from which we last made the treacherous dive. As we developed confidence mixed with questionable judgment, we dared to dive from a higher point on the rock ledges each time we visited the island. I would venture to say we left off somewhere between 30 to 40 feet. It was scary and exhilarating at the same time.

Camp Lewis had an Indian honor society called "Lukamus." Initiation into the society was determined by existing members, comprised of both campers and counselors, based on being recognized as a good community citizen who exhibited qualities such as honesty, fairness, helpfulness, and caring kindness. During each one-month camp session, there was an initiation date. We did not know which campers and counselors would be chosen as we stood in a circle for roll call before lunch. With no warning, a band of Lukamus members dressed in full Indian garb including feathered headdresses would come out of hiding and, with startlingly loud hoots and hollers, run around the circle of campers and counselors. One at a time, they would push into the middle of the circle those who were chosen as Lukamus initiates. This event was followed by a four-day initiation that included spending a night alone in the forest with only one match with which to start a warm campfire.

I remember my initiation into the Lukamus honor society. The recognition was not only a self-esteem boost and validation of my personality, but it also synchronized with my identity as a person of the Earth, a global citizen and steward of nature. Once initiated, one could carve a set of Lukamus beads to wear on the wrist as evidence of membership. There are three beads, each one painted in yellow, red, or blue, and strung on a leather lanyard. It was a meticulous procedure to make an enduring set of Lukamus beads, and I made mine to perfection. The summer after I was accepted, my brother, Marc, was also initiated. I was really proud and relieved of the guilt I felt about being in the inner circle without him.

I now live in Vermont for which I credit my childhood summers at Lac Beauchamp in the Laurentian Mountains. I bonded with nature during those childhood summers, which gave me solace and hope in contrast to my traumatic experiences in New York City. Science has now validated nature as a healing force for all manner of conditions, including anxiety and depression. When I teach mental health workshops for therapists, educators, and other professionals, I always ask, "Where do you like to go on vacations?" Invariably, audience members say, "mountains," "beach," "ocean," or "lakes." I then ask, "What is it about those nature settings that draws you to them?" The replies include "peaceful," "calming," and "restorative." But there is one other reason that hardly anyone mentions: Nature humbles us as we realize our place in the big picture of life. The mountains, lakes, and ocean were here before we were, and they will be here long after we are gone. In other words, spending time in nature is "perspective changing" and helps us realize that our troubles and worries are small in the larger scheme of life.

CHAPTER 3

New Haven, Connecticut

(1964–1968)

WHEN MY MOTHER DROPPED ME OFF at Yale to begin my freshman year, I thought I had landed on another planet. I was surrounded by wealth the likes of which I had never seen before in one place. There were certainly some other students who, like me, were on financial scholarships, but many were "legacy students" from wealthy families. I remember one classmate who told me he was a 13th-generation Yalie, meaning that his family had sent 13 consecutive generations of offspring to the college.

As evidence of their wealth, many Yale students wore expensive blue blazers and Harris Tweed jackets. Some had sports cars and shiny black BMW motorcycles with white pinstripes. I dreamed I would someday have a BMW motorcycle and, 32 years later, I got the first of four successive BMW RTs (Road Tourers). My current bike is a wonder of modern technology, with ABS brakes, cruise control, heated seats, heated hand grips, and the proprietary horizontally opposed twin-cylinder engine that makes the brand unique. The bike has 130 horsepower and can go from 0 to 60 mph in 4.2 seconds. It's a thrill to ride and always makes me smile. I've also had my share of Harris Tweed sports jackets and blue blazers, which I love to wear with blue jeans.

The Freshman Commons was a housing complex consisting mostly of quads, with four students in a shared apartment with two bedrooms and a living area. I opted for one of the few doubles, which

I shared with my roommate, Anthony, from New Jersey. Anthony had diabetes, and I was in awe of how he calmly gave himself an insulin injection in his leg every morning. Each complex had a resident adviser, typically a graduate student whose housing was provided in exchange for being an on-site resource for personal issues such as relationship conflicts or academic decision-making.

There were 1,000 freshmen in my class, so it was easy to feel lost in the crowd. The freshman dining hall was huge and I had a work-study job, which Yale called a "bursary job," that required me to pour orange juice behind the line as well as to bus the tables. It was embarrassing, and I felt like a servant to the more advantaged students. I discussed my feelings with the resident adviser, who solved the matter by suggesting I take out a student loan equivalent to the dollar value of the work-study job. When I told the dining hall manager of my decision, he said he knew it was a demeaning job and he completely understood and supported my decision. Giving up the dining hall job freed up some time to devote to studying at Yale's demanding academic program. I was also training as a member of the track team and I found it overwhelming to manage all of those commitments simultaneously. In the evenings, when I planned to study, I would usually put my head on the library table and fall asleep.

It took me almost two years to come into my own at Yale. I was surrounded by smart people who learned how to study and take exams at private New England high schools such as Andover and Hotchkiss. In high school, I was a big fish in a small pond, but at Yale I was in the company of the big fish from all around the world. By the end of the second year, I made the Dean's List and thereafter achieved Ranking Scholar, which was defined as being in the top 10 percent of the class.

I planned to major in architecture at Yale's acclaimed School of Art and Architecture, but I switched to psychology after a course in personality and social psychology taught by Professor Mike Kahn. Amazingly, many years later when I was established as a clinical psychologist, one of my interns came to a supervision session carrying a book in her hand. When I inquired about what she was reading, she handed me a book about psychotherapy written by none other than Mike Kahn.

Yale is an institution with a long history dating back to 1638 with the founding of the New Haven Colony by a band of 500 Puritans who fled persecution in England. It was the dream of Reverend John Davenport, the religious leader of the colony, to establish a theocracy and a college to educate its leaders. Yale College opened in 1701 as an all-male seminary.

When I attended Yale, it was still an all-male college and a formal environment where a coat and tie were required in the dining halls. I started a vintage tie craze that met the attire requirement with brightly colored, wide silk ties that I would pick up for pennies at vintage stores in New York City and sell to classmates at Yale. It was a spoof on formality and an expression of the antiauthoritarianism of my youth.

Yale became coed in 1968, just after I graduated. That was unfortunate for me considering my general distrust of men as well as my tendency to feel out of place as a scholarship student. I coped by spending virtually every weekend in Greenwich Village with my high school girlfriend. I took the New Haven railroad train directly to Penn Station in Manhattan followed by a few stops on the subway to the West Fourth Street station. A short walk led me to her apartment in the Village.

On a few occasions, I rode from New Haven to New York City in the passenger seat of a classmate's sports car. Andy was from the Upper East Side of Manhattan, an upscale area known for expensive

housing with doormen. Andy's convertible MG sports car was one
symbol of his family's wealth. I shared the cost of gas and tolls, and I
have vivid memories of cruising down the Merritt Parkway on Friday
afternoons with the wind in my face. Andy would perfunctorily drop
me off at a subway station near his house and I would take the train
down to Greenwich Village. I do not remember driving back to New
Haven with Andy. I usually took the train back on Monday mornings.

Since I felt out of place at Yale and spent so little time on campus,
I made only one or two lasting friendships. One was Ron, a Mexican
American architecture major who came to Yale from Washington,
D.C. He, too, was a scholarship student and could identify with how
I felt. I remember him telling me about the advice his father, a govern-
ment worker, gave him regarding how to survive in a bureaucratic job:
"Walk quickly and carry papers." Ron and I vowed we would never
take a job as a government worker in a bureaucracy. After earning a
bachelor's degree in 1968, Ron stayed on at Yale's School of Art and
Architecture and obtained a master's degree. He then moved to San
Francisco where he worked as an architect and city planner. He also
taught at the City College of San Francisco. We kept in touch until
2013 when I learned that he died after an eight-month battle with
brain cancer. Having also lost my grandparents, parents, a brother,
aunt and uncle, and my childhood friend Raymond, I began to see
that life involves an inevitable series of losses. But again, if we think
of relationships as serving a purpose, we can internalize and carry with
us the lessons and learning gained from each relationship.

For social life, Yale hosted weekend mixers. Female students from
Vassar and Smith, both all-women colleges at the time, were bused
in for outrageous parties with live bands and endless kegs of beer. For
lack of a better term, these were out-of-control, drunken *orgies* that
turned me off. At the last so-called mixer I attended, I watched with

dismay as the bandleader dry-humped an intoxicated female student on the stage.

To earn money during the summers, I worked as a house painter. For some reason, perhaps because I am tall with long arms, I was proficient at painting and I developed skills in both interior and exterior painting. I also have a tendency toward perfectionism, so my work was both quick and of high quality. During one summer, I also worked full time as an electrician's helper. My job involved loading and unloading the mechanics' trucks, hauling spools of cable, drilling holes for electrical circuits in homes under construction, installing outlet boxes and fishing wire through existing homes when additional lighting or other electrical upgrades were needed. I used a power drill that must have weighed 25 pounds, not counting the 36-inch-long wood bits. I also learned how to repair lamps and electrical appliances. I acquired a set of electrician's hand tools and I watched other tradesmen contribute their part to new construction houses. They included plumbers, heating and air-conditioning installers, and "rockers." The rockers were Sheetrock experts; I was amazed at how they could walk around a house on stilts to reach the ceilings when it came time for joint compounding. Sheetrock requires three applications of compound on all seams and Sheetrock screws, each separated by at least 24 hours of drying time.

The summer jobs taught me the skills that would prove to be valuable later in life. Many years later, while living in Vermont, I remodeled and built six homes. The improvements and sweat equity involved in these ventures led to significant financial rewards with each sale. I was able to leverage the value of the homes to finance college educations for my two daughters and build my current home, a solar-powered house with 41 windows overlooking a nature preserve. The home has views of Mount Mansfield, Vermont's tallest mountain, to the east, and the Adirondack Mountains to the west.

The skills I acquired during those summer jobs while at Yale also resulted in a significant boost to my self-esteem. As it turns out, improved self-esteem contributes immensely to trauma recovery. Self-esteem develops from two sources: positive input from primary caregivers early in life and experiences of competence, success, and mastery (such as problem solving and acquiring new skills). I did not have an abundance of positive input as a child, but the skills I learned gave me confidence that I could learn to be successful in life. Moreover, the physical skills I learned helped me feel good about my body. New research on trauma finds a common symptom of post-traumatic stress disorder is *dissociation*: We "leave our bodies" as a way of coping with painful feelings. In *The Body Keeps the Score: Brain, Mind and Body in the Healing of Trauma* (2014), psychiatrist Bessel van der Kolk suggests that we need to *reinhabit* our bodies as part of recovery. The combination of success in athletics and acquiring many physical skills were certainly instrumental in my trauma recovery.

Yale provided me with an extraordinary liberal arts education. I was impressed by the professors who were masters in their fields, such as Margaret Mead in anthropology and Vincent Scully in art history. As a senior, I coauthored a psychology study that was published in the peer-reviewed *Journal of Personality and Social Psychology*. That study shaved a year off my PhD program when I was able to obtain credit for the equivalent of a master's thesis. Socially, however, Yale was probably not the best choice for me given my trauma history. At Yale, I was surrounded by men, many of whom were from another social class, and it was never comfortable. Had Yale been a coed university when I was a student there, I would likely have had an entirely different experience.

CHAPTER 4

Montreal, Quebec

(1968–1969)

I WAS A SENIOR AT YALE when the Selective Service System terminated the student deferment and instituted the lottery system, all designed to conscript more young men into the military during the Vietnam War. College students during the Vietnam War considered a variety of ways to avoid the draft. Some found ways to "fail" their physical exam when their number came up in the lottery. One classmate planned to swallow the whites of 40 eggs the night before the physical exam in hopes that his urine would have the consistency suggestive of alcoholism. The scheme apparently worked, as he did fail the physical exam and was exempted from serving in the military. Others left the United States and emigrated to Canada. A few signed up in hopes of securing a desk job.

The Vietnam War was actually a civil war between North Vietnam and South Vietnam. North Vietnam was supported by the communist countries of Russia and China, while South Vietnam was supported by the U.S., Australia, the Philippines, and other anti-communist allies. The U.S. military entered this conflict without congressional approval. Our country was deeply divided and there was a vigorous anti-war movement with large public demonstrations and even a number of citizens who, in protest, publicly burned themselves to death. In the end we lost some 58,000 men and women, and one of the tragedies of the war was that surviving soldiers were too often met with disdain and dishonor upon their return. In addition to lost U.S troops, it is estimated that as many as 2 million Vietnamese civilians on both sides died and 1.1 million North Vietnamese and Viet Cong soldiers were killed.

When my lottery number was called, I passed my draft physical and was in line to serve in the military. I planned to apply for a conscientious objector classification, which I knew would be difficult to obtain. The conscientious objector classification would result in a requirement to work for two years engaged in "civilian service in the national interest." However, as a backup plan, I applied to and was accepted to the PhD program in clinical psychology at McGill University in Montreal. I was familiar with Montreal as my parents were born and raised there as Canadian citizens, and I spent time there as a child. I became a "landed immigrant" in Canada, the first step toward establishing residency and ultimately Canadian citizenship. I started the doctoral program at McGill in 1968.

For the first year in Montreal, I rented an apartment at 125 Milton Street, which was within walking distance to the university. The PhD program was housed in the Biological Sciences Building. I recall that my adviser, a psychologist named Marcel, would drive his car from an underground garage at his apartment building to the underground parking lot below the Biological Sciences Building. It appeared that his life was lived completely indoors, and I thought to myself, "This is not how I want to live."

Before I moved to Montreal to start the PhD program, I met Nancy. We were both counselors at a summer day camp for disadvantaged children in New York City. I was still a senior at Yale, but I spent the year living in the Bronx near a residential treatment school in Hawthorne, where I was working part-time as a recreational counselor. I was doing independent study as a Yale senior and did not need to be in residence at the college in New Haven. Nancy, who was an elementary school teacher, moved in with me and we were subsequently married in 1968 after I graduated from Yale. The wedding was outdoors in Pearl River, New York, in a posh community on the New Jersey side of the Hudson River. Unfortunately, the decision to marry was driven by time pressure when I was accepted at McGill and poised to leave the country.

Nancy's parents were clearly wealthy, but their relationship was dysfunctional and the tension between them was palpable. Ultimately, Nancy's mother moved to Miami where she had a relationship with a man who owned a residential treatment center. To help her move, I drove her convertible Ford Mustang from New York City to Miami, a drive that included a speeding ticket at a speed trap in Georgia. That was prior to the completion of Interstate 95 through the southern states along the Eastern Seaboard. I was clocked at just a few miles over the 60-mph speed limit, and I was instructed to follow the police car to a local judge's house where I paid the fine in lieu of jail. The parking lot at the judge's house was full of out-of-state cars with disgusted drivers who were also picked up at the speed trap. It was obviously a racket for local income.

I was lucky to not get caught speeding on one particular drive to Montreal. I had to spend a few days at McGill before returning to New York City for my scheduled conscientious objector interview at my local draft board. Nancy's father offered me his Cadillac to drive up to Montreal and back, a one-way distance of 385 miles. I drove at night and made the trip in four and a half hours, *averaging* 90 mph on the Adirondack Northway, a new section of the New York State Thruway between Albany and the Canadian border. Driving the Cadillac at night was surreal, like driving a living room couch in outer space. At speeds near 100 mph there is no margin for error: Drifting out of your lane could easily result in death. There were no car seat belts or air bags in 1968. After avoiding death by car crash, I showed up for my conscientious objector interview with my draft board in New York City.

A conscientious objector is a person who is opposed to serving in the armed forces or bearing arms on the grounds of moral or religious principles. A registrant making a claim for conscientious objector status is required to appear before his local draft board to explain his beliefs. He may provide written documentation to support his claim or include witnesses who might attest to his claims. A written statement is required to explain how he arrived at his beliefs and the influence his beliefs had on how he lives his life. I took all of these steps and I still have the written application I filed at the tender age of 21.

To be asked as a 21-year-old man to justify my objection to war and military conscription, as well as to provide references and witnesses, was challenging. Nevertheless, I stepped up to the process, which included answering questions posed on the conscientious objector application. Here are two sample questions and my responses:

Question: Describe the nature of your belief which is the basis of your claim, and state whether or not your belief in a Supreme Being involves duties which to you are superior to those arising from any human relation.

My response: I do not believe in an anthropomorphic supreme being. I believe, however, that the rightness of valuing human life and the wrongness of taking human life constitutes a higher standard of behavior than the command of others who would place me in a position which directly or indirectly requires me to take the lives of human beings. This ideal brings me to the position where the value of human life transcends the instructions of any one individual or group to participate in any form of activity involving the destruction of human life. It is a conscientious objection to war in the light of a higher standard which prevents me from accepting a military status of any kind. I cannot remain faithful to my conscience and at the same time participate in war of any kind because I believe in an ideal which holds that it is wrong, morally and ethically, to take human life. I cannot abandon my conscience to help equip my government for waging war, for taking life. I would instead invest myself—my intelligence, my understanding, and my compassion—in working towards human potential and a better community of man.

Question: Under what circumstances, if any, do you believe in the use of force?

My response: "Force" is generally defined as "constraint or resistance exerted upon or against someone or something." I would make a distinction between "force" and "violence," the latter denoting hostility in the exercise of force. I cannot support violence under any circumstances. This does not mean, however, that under some circumstances I would not be forceful.

I believe in the use of force against someone who posed an immediate threat of physical injury to myself, my family, or another human being. On the other hand, I would only consider the use of force to constrain another or others if I perceived and believed at that moment that my behavior might prevent the loss of human life, and with the intent to help another whose life was physically in danger. I have in the past and I would, if necessary, use my physical strength to save the life of another person. For example, if a person were drowning, I would use force to rescue the person even if the person instinctively resisted my aid. I would also use force to resist an inanimate object that threatened someone's life. If an automobile was rolling towards someone, for example, I would use force in an attempt to arrest the automobile, or I would push the person away from the automobile in an attempt to save his or her life.

The application process was traumatic and my anxiety was peaking. I was already feeling like an expatriate as a resident in Canada, and I felt my U.S. citizenship and entire future was on the line with the conscientious objector application. Furthermore, U.S. involvement in the Vietnam War, which I considered to be immoral and illegitimate, was in itself traumatic. The real-time evening news was almost exclusively focused on the war and it was like a violent video game, with rising death counts not unlike the 2020 to 2021 news reports of coronavirus pandemic deaths.

There were two types of conscientious objector designations, and acceptable service was determined by the individual's specific beliefs. The person opposed to any form of military service would be assigned to civilian service in the national interest. The person whose beliefs allowed him to serve in the military but in a noncombatant capacity would serve without combat training or duties that included using weapons. The second type described my father, who joined the U.S. Army to fight against Hitler and served as a medic during World War II.

I prevailed with the draft board and was given the noncombatant conscientious objector status. I started planning a return to the U.S. from Canada to perform the required two years of alternative service. The Selective Service System had a state-by-state list of alternative service employers, consisting mostly of nonprofit organizations such as the Salvation Army and Goodwill services. However, other types of jobs were possible if they were deemed to make a meaningful contribution to maintenance of the national health, safety, and interest. Examples of alternative service jobs would be work in conservation, caring for the very young or old, education, and health care.

My Angel Theory of Relationships was evident when I was offered a job in Miami at the residential treatment center owned by Nancy's mother's partner. I was able to obtain approval for the job as a health care provider using my psychology skills. Many of the children at the treatment center were wards of the state from which they were sent to treatment, and some were dependents of active military personnel. That phase of my story is the subject of the following chapter.

CHAPTER 5

Miami, Florida

(1969–1970)

AFTER COMPLETING MY FIRST YEAR in the PhD program in clinical psychology at McGill University in Montreal, and with consent from my draft board in New York City, I relocated with Nancy to Florida where I would start my conscientious objector service. I would be working as a residential supervisor at the Montanari Residential Treatment Center.

What made an immediate impression on me was Florida's lush vegetation, sweet fragrance of honeysuckle, plentiful sunshine, and warm, tropical air. There were tall coconut trees everywhere as well as an amazing variety of cactus plants. Combined with the sandy beaches and salty ocean breezes, it felt like paradise. It was a far cry from the cold and gray winter I had just endured in Montreal.

The treatment center, which consisted of a series of group homes, was located in Hialeah, a suburb of Miami. But I wanted to live near the ocean and found a cottage to rent on Key Biscayne. There I could go for runs along the beach and swim in the ocean. The nearest town was Coconut Grove, a hip community with ethnic restaurants, art galleries, and outdoor festivals. I became familiar with Cuban cuisine, including red beans and rice as well as fried and sugared plantains.

The drive to work took about 20 minutes on a circumferential highway that skirted Miami. The treatment center consisted of an administration building, where I had an office as the residential supervisor, and about eight houses with day and night shift "house parents." I was responsible for the staff and residential life of the children and teens, whereas there was a school program managed by a counterpart education director. The children, who were mostly delinquent youngsters who were abused or neglected in their home states, could best be described as angry and distrustful. They frequently acted out aggressively or attempted suicide by overdosing with their medication. I made numerous trips to the local hospital emergency rooms to have their stomachs pumped out when it was not too late to rescue them. The treatment center was a last-resort effort to help these victims of childhood abuse and neglect.

On my first day on the job, a group of teens who looked like a gang challenged me. The leader of the pack confronted me as to who I was and why I was there. I knew this was a test and my response would have a lasting effect on my success as the residential supervisor. I kept my cool, showed interest in the alpha leader, and found a way to befriend him and pass the test. I was relieved when he turned to the group and said, "He's OK . . . he's cool."

I was also tested by some of the staff, especially the veteran house parents who saw me as an impudent young person who was over his head as a supervisor. In truth, I did not have much experience as a supervisor other than being a summer camp tribe director responsible for other counselors. It took a while to earn the respect of the house parents and have them see me as a supportive ally. I represented them to the administration, especially to the facility's owner, when it came to matters of salary and benefits.

Many couples without children have pets they treat like children. In some cases, raising a pet, such as a puppy, is one way a couple can explore how they would work together as parents and share responsibility for a dependent, living being. For these reasons, Nancy and I acquired an Irish setter puppy in Florida we named Sean. Like many couples, we treated Sean like our child. Since dogs and cats were not permitted in the Amsterdam Houses in which I grew up, I did not have any experience with a pet other than a parakeet and some goldfish. We really did not know how to train a puppy and Sean was both a joy and a source of frustration. Irish setters are high-energy hunting dogs and they need to run. I took Sean for runs on the beach, but he needed more. I sometimes drove my car along the beach with Sean running alongside as the only way I could get him tired enough to make it through a day without chewing our shoes or furniture, particularly while we were out of the house or at work.

I bought my first-ever new car in Miami, a beige 1969 Volkswagen Beetle with a four-speed stick shift, wooden steering wheel, and a sunroof. I viewed it as a sports car and drove it as though it was, even though it had only an air-cooled, 53 horsepower engine compared to the popular muscle cars of the era—Ford Mustangs, Chevy Camaros, and Pontiac Firebirds—with engines having as much as 450 horsepower. The good news is that the Volkswagen Beetle averaged 32 miles per gallon and the cost of gasoline averaged 23 cents per gallon. In 1969, the Beetle cost $1,799 new.

At that time, cars needed an oil change every 2,000 miles as well as valve adjustments, new spark plugs, rotors, and distributor caps at least every 5,000 miles. I had no car mechanic skills but wanted to learn how to maintain my vehicle. I am indebted to a guy named Mike Campbell, who ran the maintenance shop and industrial arts program at the Montanari Residential Treatment Center. Mike took me to a Sears Department Store where I acquired my first set of wrenches, feeler gauges, and other tools for servicing a car. Mike showed me how to replace the engine oil, tune the engine, and keep the car running optimally. He was another angel in my life.

Another angel was Karen, a single woman my age who worked as a day shift house parent at the treatment center. Housing at the facility was a benefit for day shift house parents so I saw her frequently. As I was married to Nancy, Karen and I developed a close but nonsexual relationship and she remains a friend to this day, 50 years later. Karen left Florida and drove to California as a passenger with a friendly lesbian couple and started a new life in Los Angeles. I subsequently connected her with Saul Neidorf, my training analyst and friend from my time in San Francisco, and his wife, Anne-Marie. The Neidorfs, who had no children together, virtually adopted Karen as a daughter. As such, Karen was identified in their wills as the executrix of their estate. The Neidorfs were undoubtedly angels in my life who treated me as a son. In effect, Karen is like a sister to me. See Chapter 6 for details of my angel relationship with this surrogate family.

San Francisco, California

(1970–1971)

ALTHOUGH MY TIME IN MIAMI served the purpose of fulfilling a year of my alternative service as a conscientious objector, I felt that I was losing time as a doctoral student in clinical psychology. In an effort to resume my doctoral training, I obtained and compared two listings: one was a list of employers approved by the Selective Service System for conscientious objectors, and the other was a list of predoctoral internships in clinical psychology that were approved by the American Psychological Association (APA). One match stood out to me as an opportunity to continue my conscientious objector obligation while also fulfilling the predoctoral internship requirement. It was a formal, one-year internship at the Department of Psychiatry at Mount Zion Hospital in San Francisco, California. "A perfect match," I thought. Under normal circumstances, the internship is done as the last year in APA-approved PhD programs, but I had completed only the first year at McGill. Nevertheless, I decided to apply to the internship. To my surprise and delight, I was accepted for one of only three openings out of hundreds of applicants. The internship would begin in September 1970.

But there was a problem. I discovered that as a conscientious objector working in Florida, my alternative service was under the jurisdiction of the Florida draft board rather than my original draft board in New York City. I was shocked and dismayed when the

Florida board would not release me. It simply made no sense that I would be prevented from changing alternative service settings when both met the government's published requirements. I appealed the decision and ultimately prevailed, but it took several months to resolve during which the September start time in San Francisco was slipping away. How did I handle this bind? I provided regular updates to the internship director at Mount Zion Hospital. I distinctly remember his name: Dr. Don Cliggett. Amazingly, Dr. Cliggett offered to defer my acceptance to the following September, almost a year away! This would allow me enough time to resolve the conscientious objector matter with the Florida draft board. I can only conclude that Dr. Cliggett was another angel in my life.

I recently learned that Dr. Cliggett died in 2017. His obituary states that he grew up in Brooklyn, New York, and received his PhD in psychology from New York University. He moved to San Francisco in 1965 to join the "dynamic psychoanalytic community at Mount Zion Hospital (the very place I was going for training) where he spent a joyful 33 years teaching and training interns in psychology."

Nancy and I left Miami in the Volkswagen Beetle with all our worldly possessions on board including Sean, our Irish setter. We drove 1,800 miles north to New York City to visit our families before heading west on the 3,000-mile drive to San Francisco.

The very first thing I saw when I got out of the car on Van Ness Avenue in the heart of San Francisco were two men walking and openly smoking marijuana. Similar to my experience when I arrived at Yale years ago, I felt like I had just landed on another planet. Miami was a politically conservative city in a Republican state, whereas San Francisco was a progressive city in a Democratic state. The idea that people could smoke marijuana publicly in 1968 was simply astounding. This was of interest in that I had already been introduced to marijuana and found it helpful in my trauma recovery. I felt relaxed for the first time in my life when I used it.

We were able to find an apartment to rent in the Castro Valley section of San Francisco, a 15-minute drive to Mount Zion Hospital on Divisadero Street where I would be starting my predoctoral internship in psychology. Like New York City, San Francisco is densely populated and there were elements of danger and crime in most sections of the city. For example, one of the psychiatry residents was mugged and robbed while walking to the hospital from his parked car on a nearby side street. Since I grew up in New York City, I was accustomed to being vigilantly aware of threats in my environment.

Mount Zion Hospital and Medical Center was a training hospital, and the mental health program was housed in the Department of Psychiatry. During my year there from September 1970 to September 1971, there were a dozen residents in psychiatry, several trainees in clinical social work, and three predoctoral clinical psychology interns. Besides me, the two other psychology interns were Harriet and Steve Lerner. Harriet went on to write a series of books, including *The Dance of Fear* (2009), *The Dance of Intimacy* (2009), and *The Dance of Anger* (2014). It is interesting to note that both Harriet and I independently went on to write books about anxiety using the dance metaphor. My first book was *Dancing With Fear: Overcoming Anxiety in a World of Stress and Uncertainty* (1996), published more than a decade before Harriet's first book. Steve was a hobby musician who built a recording studio using cardboard egg cartons for sound deadening. Steve and Harriet went on to spend their professional careers at the Menninger Foundation, a prominent psychiatric hospital and treatment center located at that time in Topeka, Kansas.

The trainees at Mount Zion's Department of Psychiatry participated together in weekly case conferences focused on child and adult psychotherapy. In addition, as a psychology intern, I had five weekly, individual supervision sessions in the following specialties: child psychotherapy, psychological testing of children, adult psychotherapy, psychological testing of adults, and group therapy. The supervision was provided by practicing clinicians. The setting was a rich learning environment in which training was provided in a psychoanalytic framework. The training model was consultative: We each had a caseload of patients we would see independently in our offices followed by the weekly supervision meetings to review our cases and discuss our work. We were trusted to work autonomously with patients assigned to us.

The primary approach to psychotherapy at that time was psychoanalytic, a modified form of traditional psychoanalysis. The approach was considered the gold standard for counseling into the 1970s. Techniques such as cognitive behavioral therapy (CBT), exposure and response prevention (ERP), mindfulness, eye movement desensitization and reprocessing (EMDR), dialectical behavioral therapy (DBT), acceptance and commitment therapy (ACT), and other approaches had not yet been developed. It was believed that insight—understanding the source of one's symptoms—was sufficient for symptom reduction. But insight is not always transformative. Indeed, even Freud, the founder of psychoanalysis believed that insight alone is like giving a dinner menu only to a hungry person. In other words, even Freud recognized the limits of the psychoanalytic approach to therapy.

The training program was intense and my mind was spinning with new information and learning. What made the training even more powerful is that each of the three psychology interns was offered the opportunity to have a personal analysis. Therapy would be provided free of charge by psychiatrists as a condition of their faculty membership in the Department of Psychiatry. All three of us opted to accept the offer, and I was assigned to Dr. Saul Neidorf for my personal analysis.

Saul turned out to be another angel in my life. He was a warm, authentic, and down-to-earth therapist, unlike some of the other psychiatrists who were formal, mechanical, and traditional. We met at least twice per week for more than a year and we covered a lot of ground in terms of my family history, trauma, and anxiety. Saul was the first person with whom I shared the horror story of the childhood abuse, some 10 years after those traumatic experiences. Saul helped me immensely and, as I mentioned in Chapter 1, we remained connected until his death in 2008, long after my time in San Francisco. I honored Saul in the acknowledgments section of my first book, *Dancing With Fear*, with the following words: "I will be forever grateful to Saul Neidorf, MD, whose trusted ears were the first to hear about my painful childhood and anxiety condition. As therapist, teacher, and mentor *par excellence*, Saul demonstrated that therapy heals by shared heart, and he had a significant influence on my therapeutic style." I used the French expression, *par excellence*, knowing that Saul went to medical school in France. I acknowledged Saul again in my second book, *The Worried Child*, published in 2003, with these words: "Thanks to Saul Neidorf for helping me understand that we bring our childhood with us as we mature."

As I was doing the work in therapy, I realized that I was unhappy in my marriage with Nancy. As Nancy and I talked honestly about our feelings, it was apparent that she, too, was unhappy, and that we were drifting apart. We made the painful decision to get divorced and we walked hand in hand into a divorce attorney's office agreeing to end the marriage. In California, a couple can be granted a divorce by the court if they meet the criteria for "irreconcilable differences." We had no children and no real property other than Sean, the Irish setter. I agreed to give custody of the dog to Nancy in exchange for "visitation rights."

I was truly single for the first time since adolescence, and my anxiety about being alone was high. I functioned effectively as long as I was busy, but I would have panic attacks whenever I faced an unscheduled or open-ended weekend. My financial resources were limited to the $300 per month stipend I received from the National Institute of Mental Health as an intern and graduate student. I first took a room in a depressing boarding house, and then put up a "Seeking Housing" notice on the bulletin board at Mount Zion Hospital. This resulted in my meeting John Lyons, another angel in my life.

John referred to himself as "the hospital TV man." Patients in those days had to pay extra for a telephone or television in their rooms, and John's job was simply to install the equipment and remove it when patients were discharged. We met over lunch in the hospital cafeteria, which fortunately provided meals to trainees and employees without charge, and we made an immediate connection. We were both looking for a roommate with whom we could share an apartment. We proceeded to find and rent a second-floor flat in a duplex owned by a sweet older woman who lived on the first level. It was on Noe Street, again in the Castro Valley area of San Francisco.

John was the most relaxed, *mellow* person I had ever met. After our first dinner together, John got up from the table and said to me, "Don't call me, I'll call you," as he went into his bedroom. After several evenings with the same scenario, I asked him what he was doing in his room. "I meditate," John explained. When I told John that I was interested in learning how to meditate, especially if it could help me relax, he offered to teach me.

John was a Sufi practitioner. Sufism is a Middle Eastern form of spirituality in which meditation and "whirling Dervish dancing" were practiced as a path to enlightenment. John demonstrated how he would sit upright on a dining room chair, close his eyes, and focus on a special word, which I learned was called a mantra. The mantra he used was given to him by his guru, a spiritual teacher named Samuel Lewis who had a following in San Francisco. I had the good fortune to attend some of the Sufi gatherings, practice meditation with them, and witness their ecstatic form of dancing.

John helped me understand the practice of meditation. By focusing on a single word or object such as a candle flame (John was big on candles and had numerous brass candleholders), the mind could train itself to disregard the many thoughts that distract us, cause distress, and interfere with our ability to experience a calm state of mind. I realized meditation was the practice that allowed John to be so peaceful, mellow, and easygoing. I started practicing meditation in earnest, scheduling two 20-minute sessions per day as prescribed by John as well as the books I was reading on transcendental meditation.

It was extremely difficult for me to sit still and focus on a mantra as I was easily distracted by incessant thoughts and an active mind. With John's encouragement, I stayed with it and began to experience the benefits of the practice. I began to feel calmer and more engaged in the present moment, as compared to planning and worrying about the future. Other people noticed this gradual change and gave me feedback on how relaxed I seemed to be. I believe that meditation practice helped me develop the laser focus that has allowed me to achieve so much in my life, such as completing my PhD and writing four previous books on the topic of anxiety. Any project or goal that cannot be accomplished in a short period of time requires the ability to sustain focus and resist the pull of so many competing distractions.

Apart from his job at the hospital, John had a metalworks business specializing in brass. He had a shop in which he repaired and sold brass objects including brass beds, and he could restore the luster to anything made of metal. Unfortunately, five years after I completed my predoctoral internship and left San Francisco to return to graduate school, I learned that John had been murdered. The police report reads that a gunman entered his metalsmith shop through a back door with two hostages taken after robbing a printing shop next door. The hostages, who apparently lived through the ordeal, testified that the gunman shot John at close range without provocation. My heart broke when I learned about this tragic end to John's life. How could such a kind, generous, and peaceful man be killed in cold blood? There is no doubt that life involves losses, some more tragic and unnatural than others.

As a young, single, professional man in San Francisco, I had no trouble meeting people including eligible women. I dated frequently, as though I was making up for lost time. I had numerous relationships ranging in duration from one night to several months. I also started practicing yoga, which was compatible with my meditation practice, and I met many interesting people in the active spiritual community of the Bay area.

One significant relationship was with an attractive, artistic woman named Liz. As her day job, Liz worked as a receptionist at Mount Zion Hospital where I was in training. She cleverly sent someone to tell me she was interested in meeting me, and I happily responded. For our first date, I invited her to take a motorcycle ride with me around the San Francisco Bay Area and down the scenic Pacific Coast Highway. I will never forget the feeling of riding open air with an attractive woman hugging me around the waist. We subsequently spent a lot of time together and, as another angel in my life, she introduced me to Buddhism. I still have the book she gave me as a gift, *The Way of Zen*, by Alan Watts, who was an American Buddhist and one of the first to introduce Buddhism to the American spiritual community.

My motorcycle was a 1969 Triumph "Tiger" 650 cc bike with a kick-starter. I bought it used and I was never sure how many kicks would be needed to start the engine but once it ignited, I found riding it to be exciting and blissful. I remember showing the bike to Saul, who remarked, "It's good to see that you have a pillion seat for passengers. You are not meant to be alone."

Liz had her own small business making leather neckties for men and leather accessories for women. She was clearly a talented artist and craftsperson, perhaps attributable to her mother, who was also creative and had published a cookbook with beautiful photographs. At the end of my internship in San Francisco, as I was poised to move to Nashville to continue my PhD degree, I invited Liz to go with me. As she was a person with a clear sense of identity, as well as a commitment to her business and family in the Bay area, she declined. Nevertheless, we remained connected for many years, visiting when we could, but eventually we went our separate ways. Liz ultimately got married and had children, as did I. I remember Saul saying to me when I was leaving San Francisco without Liz, "Geography is destiny!" By this he was warning me that long-distance relationships are challenging and usually do not last. I objected to the idea, believing that true love can pass the test of time and distance, but in retrospect, I must agree that he was right.

Another angel in my life was Jim, a bearded clinical social work intern at the Department of Psychiatry. Jim came to San Francisco from New Orleans where he obtained his master's in social work from Tulane University. He was happy to be in a politically progressive community as compared to Louisiana, which he viewed as a repressive, intolerant part of the South. Jim and I conversed often, discussing philosophy and psychology. We had a pattern of spending Friday nights at his house in San Rafael, north of San Francisco, across the glorious Golden Gate Bridge. On many occasions, we used LSD or mescaline to expand our consciousness. We stayed up all night talking, listening to music, "tripping," and watching the flames in his wood-burning fireplace. I usually left in the morning after sunrise. I will never forget listening with Jim to the Beatles' *Abbey Road* album, especially the song "Here Comes the Sun" as the sun rose in Marin County. My friendship with Jim was a gift in that it was an opportunity to feel a safe brotherhood with another man. The relationship helped me heal from the trauma of abuse by men. Jim was one of the few people in my life with whom I felt comfortable revealing my trauma history. The fact that he was, like me, a therapist-in-training may have contributed to my comfort, but I think I would have otherwise trusted him with my story the same way he trusted me with his deepest feelings and concerns.

I continued to experiment with hallucinogens and psychedelics as part of my spiritual practice. These substances helped me to experience what cannot be seen, attune to subtle energies, appreciate the beauty in nature, and feel connected to all living beings. Sometimes I would use these mind-altering substances to enhance my personal meditation and yoga practices, and sometimes I would partake in social situations to share the experience with others. I recall attending a Grateful Dead concert at the famed Fillmore West in San Francisco. You could openly buy "Kool-Aid" (LSD, also known as "acid") for two dollars a cup on the street outside the venue while the police walked up and down to make sure everyone was safe. As I said at the start of this chapter, this was another planet. It was also a unique historical moment, centered in the Haight-Ashbury district of San Francisco and referred to as the period of "Flower Power," and I am grateful to have been there. At the Grateful Dead concert, where there were no seats and people sat on cushions or blankets on the wooden floor, I saw people dancing naked to the live music. When I went home from the Grateful Dead concert, still experiencing the effects of the psychedelic, I was sure I had a lucid conversation with Sean, the Irish setter.

In addition to the weekly fireside visits with Jim, I developed another weekly ritual. On most Sunday afternoons, I drove over the Golden Gate Bridge to Mount Tamalpais to hike up and meditate at the top overlooking the Pacific Ocean. Mount Tam, as it was called by the locals, was accessed from the town of Sausalito. This posh community on the waterfront facing the San Francisco Bay and the island of Alcatraz was an artsy, boutique town that reminded me of Coconut Grove near Miami, except for the weather.

As I was approaching the end of my predoctoral internship in San Francisco, which also completed my two years of service as a conscientious objector, I decided to remain in the United States rather than return to Canada. As I searched for PhD programs in clinical psychology approved by the American Psychological Association, I discovered the program at George Peabody College of Vanderbilt University in Nashville, Tennessee. I was intrigued by the work of Julius Seeman, PhD, a humanistic professor who had been publishing on the topic of "self-actualization," which was of great interest to me. Jules, as he was called, was a former student of Carl Rogers and Abraham Maslow, both of whom are considered seminal thinkers in psychology. Rogers was known for the term *unconditional positive regard*, and Maslow was known for the concept of *hierarchy of needs*. I applied to and was accepted to the doctoral program, and I made plans to move from San Francisco to Nashville.

The prospect of relocating alone to an unfamiliar part of the country where I knew no one was anxiety-arousing. I feared that a "Yankee" with dark-tanned skin, reddish beard, Afro hair style, and a car with California license plates would not be welcomed. But a higher voice told me that I should face that fear and pursue my doctoral training.

My anxiety was outweighed by my belief that a PhD in psychology would increase my chances for a fulfilling life and give my trauma history a purpose. I sold the Triumph motorcycle and set out in the VW Beetle for the next stage of the journey.

At the very same time I was leaving San Francisco, my friend from Yale, Ron, was moving to San Francisco. He was looking for housing and the timing was perfect for me to introduce him to John and to take over my room in the apartment. The timing was divinely inspired for two angels in my life to meet and live together.

CHAPTER 7

Nashville, Tennessee

(1971–1974)

I ARRIVED IN NASHVILLE after the 2,400-mile drive from San Francisco and immediately set out to find housing. One of the professors, a single man, invited me to stay temporarily as a guest at his apartment while I searched for suitable housing. I was pleasantly surprised to feel welcomed so quickly. I found the university bulletin board and saw a "For Rent" notice with a phone number. I could not have known at that moment that another angel would enter my life.

Paul and Katherine Chrisman were a salt of the earth couple who lived on the other side of the tracks from the university section of Nashville. On their lot was a small two-bedroom cottage that they were renting out for additional income. They were godparents to a young woman—a country singer-songwriter who posted the "For Rent" notice. At the appointed time, I met Paul Chrisman, who had just arrived home in an old pickup truck from his job as a cabinet maker at an industrial shop. He had long, white hair, a white beard, and, I quickly learned, a wooden leg. He stood silently for what seemed like a very long time, sizing me up before he spoke. I apparently passed the test and the Chrismans rented the cottage to me for $50 per month. The price was right as I was living on a student stipend of $300 per month from the National Institute of Mental Health.

Not long after I moved in, the Chrismans began inviting me over for dinner. I remember Katherine's salmon croquettes and peach cobbler desserts. They soon became my surrogate family and I had an opportunity to meet the musician who posted the "For Rent" notice. I remember one evening we went to a moving concert performance by the singer-songwriter, whose name I cannot recall.

The Chrismans were Old Testament–reading Christians who seemed interested in converting me from my identity as a Jewish Buddhist. They took a liking to me, knowing that the Old Testament is actually the Hebrew bible. Apart from the Old Testament connection, we had another thing in common: Paul revealed that he intentionally shot himself in the foot to avoid military service, which accounted for the wooden leg. Killing was against his religion, and he could identify with my beliefs as a conscientious objector. I consider the Chrismans to be among the angels in my life because of the care and interest they showed me. Three years later, when I completed my PhD program and was preparing to return to California, the Chrismans gave me a personalized copy of the Old Testament as a parting gift. Inscribed on the cover in gold lettering was this message: "To Paul Foxman from Paul and Katherine Chrisman." That touching gift is on my office bookshelf to this day.

Data from the APA's Center for Workforce Studies shows that women make up 76 percent of new psychology doctorates, and the doctoral program at Vanderbilt reflected that gender ratio. Moreover, most of the women graduate students were single, which meant that there were many opportunities for me to date. I do not know if I should be proud or embarrassed to say that on one occasion, as I looked around the university cafeteria, I realized that I had been intimate with every woman at the long table where we were eating. There were no hard feelings as the psychology community at Vanderbilt was influenced by Carl Rogers, who advocated for "open marriage."

At one point, I went to a leather shop in Nashville for a repair on my briefcase. The shop was owned by a sweet and gentle couple with whom I became friends. Shortly after we met, they informed me that they were closing the business and joining a spiritual community called The Farm, located 30 miles south of Nashville near a town named Summertown. When they invited me to visit, I entered another world in which 800 people were living in converted school buses and Army tents. They were a vegan commune whose spiritual teacher was Stephen Gaskin, an articulate and charismatic former U.S. Marine.

The history of The Farm is intriguing. Stephen was a counter-culture, beatnik preacher who was known for his presence in the Haight-Ashbury district of San Francisco in the 1960s. He held a weekly spiritual gathering in the city, known as Monday Night Class. During a two-year period, Stephen developed a large following who decided to leave San Francisco in search of land on which to establish a self-sufficient, vegan commune. They left in a caravan of 200 converted school buses, mail trucks, and other vehicles that took up 20 miles of highway, and they settled in Tennessee. Stephen wrote a series of books—*The Caravan* (1972), *This Season's People* (1976), *Mind at Play* (1979), *Amazing Dope Tales* (1990), *Cannabis Spirituality* (1996), and *Monday Night Class* (2005)—all of which I have read and still possess.

I visited my friends at The Farm a number of times, and was welcomed at the friendly but protective gate where I passed the test to be a guest. The Farm was self-sufficient in that it grew its own food with an emphasis on soybeans as the staple source of protein. Residents made sorghum syrup for sweetener and started a number of businesses for income, such as a soy ink print shop and soybean ice cream, which is still available in health food stores today. The Farm had a traveling band and the on-site spiritual services were musical, with dancing encouraged. The Farm also grew marijuana, which was used as a sacrament. In truth, it was a stoned community to which I could relate. I was once allowed to attend a meeting of the council, the governing body consisting of community representatives. I watched as a one-gallon jar of peyote tea was passed around the circle several times, a consciousness adjustment before the meeting began.

I was enamored with The Farm and considered joining the commune, which would have meant abandoning my PhD program. I decided to stay on my path toward what my intuition told me was my purpose in life. Years later, when I was living in Santa Monica, I received a call from The Farm. I was told that Stephen and The Farm Band were on tour and they asked if they could use my house as a base for their Southern California tour. They asked if they could park their converted Greyhound bus at my house and connect to my electricity. When Stephen and his wife, Ina May, knocked on my door, I invited them to stay in my spare bedroom, which they accepted. The next morning, I made oatmeal for them and we had a memorable conversation. Still enamored with The Farm, I asked Stephen if he would ever allow me to join the community. I was startled when he responded, "No, you can't join. You are a leader and you should start your own community." At first I felt rejected, but then I realized I was being validated as a leader in my own right. Stephen was right. I was a leader with a history that began as the oldest of three children; serving as editor of my high school yearbook and captain of my high school track team. I went on to be a team leader at the Vanderbilt Kennedy Center; cofounder of the Lake Champlain Waldorf School in Shelburne, Vermont; and ultimately founder and director of the Vermont Center for Anxiety Care in Burlington, where I have spent the last 20 years.

Ina May Gaskin, Steven's wife, initiated a national training program for midwives. The word was out that any pregnant woman who was considering abortion could come to the Farm for a home delivery and leave her baby with the community to raise the child. Furthermore, if the mother changed her mind, she could come back for her child. Ina May made history as the "mother of authentic midwifery." Her name is familiar to most midwives even today, and her book, *Spiritual Midwifery* (1975), is a classic on the subject.

The Farm commune was frequently investigated by the FBI for suspicion of "harboring criminals" and of being "violent protestors" and "communist rebels." Each of approximately eight investigations found the community to be a nonviolent group that always cooperated with authorities. According to documented reports released under the Freedom of Information Act, in one case, The Farm was harassed by overzealous local police who arrived with 100 heavily armed officers, two helicopters, and three TV networks to assault the community in the middle of the night with a bogus warrant derived from a dubious source, to search every house, business, school, church, and outbuilding for marijuana and drug paraphernalia. They discovered nothing. Members of The Farm filed a state civil action against the district attorney general and initiated a federal civil rights complaint, which was the subject of another FBI investigation in 1980.

At one point, however, The Farm was found to be growing marijuana, for which Stephen took responsibility, and he was arrested. Stephen represented himself and the case went all the way to the Supreme Court of Tennessee, where he was found guilty and sentenced to a prison sentence of one to four years, which he served. I remember reading that Stephen said when you put a preacher in prison, you have a built-in congregation. When Stephen was released, he returned to The Farm and continued leading the community. He died in 2014 at the age of 79.

One notable experience in Nashville occurred when a girlfriend from San Francisco, Nina, came to visit me. Among other activities, we planned to spend a day outdoors on the land owned by the family of another graduate student I had met at Vanderbilt University. He told me there was an unoccupied farmhouse situated on a large property, and that I was welcome to visit anytime without prior notice to him. He gave me the directions and said I would recognize the house, as it had a colorful paint job on the brick chimney done by a friend who was stoned at the time. He was right. I found the house with its chimney painted in the most colorful psychedelic design I had ever seen.

Nina and I followed a path behind the house that led to an open field on top of a hill, where seven-foot-tall spent cornstalks stood like soldiers in straight rows on a section of the field. We proceeded to ingest a psychedelic drug that Nina brought with her, and found ourselves wandering naked through the cornstalks. I do not remember whether the hallucinogen was mescaline, LSD, peyote, or psylocibin, all of which I had experimented with during my time in San Francisco. As we tripped around the idyllic field, laughing and dancing, I noticed something red moving at some distance across the field. I strained to see what it was, and it turned out to be two men walking purposefully toward another opening in the trees. We quickly put on our clothes as the two men turned toward us and slowly approached. I could see that one of them had a pole over his shoulder with a red sack at the end, and the other had a rifle. As my anxiety mounted, I became disoriented as to the path that led us to the field. In one of the strangest human interactions of my life, I learned that the two men were operating an illegal whiskey still in the woods and they were fearful that we would report them to the authorities. In turn, I was fearful that they would shoot us dead and leave us buried under the leaves in the forest. In an unusual negotiation, we promised we would tell no one and they promised not to shoot us. I distinctly recall the man with the gun demonstrating dramatically that he intended no harm by emptying the loaded rifle and dropping the ammunition onto the ground. In turn, I repeatedly reassured the two men that we would not reveal their secret. Since I was disoriented as to how I entered the field, the two men offered to lead us down the path to the house with the psychedelic chimney. We all stopped several times for further negotiations as they needed additional reassurance that we would not report them, and we needed additional reassurance that they would not shoot us.

I am amazed at how lasting relationships can begin in a single, unexpected moment, like the friends I made when meeting the couple at their leather shop. Another example occurred as a graduate student in Nashville. I had occasion to visit the dean's office on an academic matter and was greeted by a woman about my age who worked as the dean's administrative assistant. Her first name was MaryRuth, but she went by "MR." She had big, bright eyes and a friendly, engaging smile. After I left the office, MR contacted me and invited me to go with her to a music concert. I happily agreed and we went out on our first date, which led to a long-term angel relationship. Unfortunately, MR's father was a formal, shirt-and-tie professor at Vanderbilt University who was not happy about his daughter dating a man with California license plates, and who would probably not settle in Nashville, and who might take his daughter away. Nevertheless, MR and I were in love. I remained in Nashville for an extra year to be with MR after I obtained my PhD and license to practice psychology in Tennessee. During that year, MR and I moved in together, and thereafter she came with me when I moved back to California. Her father's fear was confirmed.

MR and I lived together for four years, three of which were in Santa Monica, California, a beach community in the Los Angeles area. While still in Nashville, we replaced her stodgy sedan with a used 1971 pumpkin-orange convertible Karmann Ghia, which was Volkswagen's version of a sports car. Believe it or not, we found a way to drive it up a ramp into a U-Haul moving truck and took it to California where it was the perfect Southern California vehicle. I drove the truck, which also contained our belongings, and MR drove the Volkswagen Beetle in a caravan across the country. The challenge was to find a suitable ramp or ledge onto which we could unload the Karmann Ghia on arrival in Los Angeles. Amazingly, we were able to find the right location for backing it out of the truck without it dropping four feet to the ground.

My four-year relationship with MR was an angel relationship, but we broke up when we realized we were not in the same place regarding marriage and children. She returned to Tennessee, where she rekindled a relationship with an old boyfriend named Tom. Tom was a wounded Vietnam veteran who was paralyzed from the waist down. He lived in a wheelchair when he was not in bed. MR and I remained friends after we separated, and I am proud of our ability to avoid bitterness and to honor each other's life trajectory. I subsequently visited Tom and MR in Tennessee and spent several weeks helping make the farmhouse they bought in the country some 30 miles south of Nashville handicap-accessible. Eventually, Tom and MR managed to conceive a child and they had a daughter. Unfortunately, Tom's life span was compromised by his war injury and he died while their daughter was still young.

One of the rewards for facing my anxiety about moving alone to Nashville was that I received a lot of support for my work in the PhD program. Dr. Jules Seeman, my doctoral adviser, was also responsible for shaving a year off the program by suggesting that I convene a committee of psychology professors to examine me on the research I coauthored and published as a senior at Yale. The idea was to demonstrate that I had the skills and knowledge equivalent to a master's thesis, and the plan worked.

But more than anything, during my three years in Nashville, I developed confidence in my ability to successfully face anxiety-arousing challenges and to see long-term projects to conclusion. That seems to be a pattern in my life: I do everything in earnest and to a high standard, and I finish whatever I start. I also overcame my preconceived ideas about the South, and I learned that people are basically the same wherever they live. There are good people—and angels—everywhere.

CHAPTER 8

Santa Monica, California

(1974–1980)

SINCE LEAVING SAN FRANCISCO to resume graduate school, I planned to return to California when I completed the PhD program. I had the opportunity when I was offered a psychologist position at a mental health center in Santa Monica. It was not San Francisco, but it appealed to me in terms of warm weather near the ocean. Remembering the feeling I had when I moved from Montreal to Miami, I was happy to live again in a semitropical climate.

MR and I made the move from Nashville to Santa Monica in a U-Haul truck loaded with the pumpkin-orange convertible Karmann Ghia, our VW Beetle in tow, our meager belongings, and MR's dog, Tassajara. Tassa, as we called her, was a sweet English sheepdog named after Tassajara, a hot springs spa in California known for its healing properties. The facility is a Zen Buddhist retreat where guests alternate between sitting in the 120-degree hot springs and the ice-cold water of an adjacent running brook. The experience is believed to stimulate the immune system and heal all manner of ailments. I can personally attest to the stimulating effect, since I did have a chance to visit Tassajara Hot Springs located in the Carmel Valley of Central California.

On arrival in Santa Monica, we rented a small old house on Ocean Avenue and Fourth Street, just a few blocks from the ocean. The house had a separate, funky, one-car garage on a corner lot with a guava tree. Once a year, the guava tree produced an abundance of fruit, which I

juiced in my juice maker. The guava juice was so refreshing and ener-
gizing that I felt I was leaving my body when I drank it. I lived there
for three years.

The mental health center was under the auspices of Saint John's
Hospital, a private Catholic medical center owned by the Sisters of
Charity of Leavenworth, Kansas. The hospital was well-endowed and
the facilities were state of the art. I would work as a psychologist in the
outpatient clinic, as well as provide consultation and support to the
staff of the inpatient psychiatric unit and nurses in the emergency
department. It was a posh job that was almost too good to be true for
a new doctoral psychologist.

Saint John's Hospital had three parallel administrations: the Sisters
of Charity, who wore traditional habits; the medical staff with a medical director; and the lay administrators known as the "bean counters."
The administration was so bureaucratic that it took months to obtain
approval for any proposed project or special request. For example, I
proposed that the hospital institute a recycling program, which was
a new idea at that time. Until then, all paper reports and other paper
products were simply shredded and put into the trash. It took several
months to convince the hospital to implement the program, which
was finally allowed on a tentative, experimental basis. In this early
effort to recycle, colored paper had to be separated from white paper,
and all staples and paper clips had to be removed. Initially, some staff
resisted these extra steps but the program was successful. In fact, the
shredded paper became a source of income as it was sold to a company
for the next step in manufacturing recycled paper goods.

Another example of organizational bureaucracy at the hospital
was the inordinate amount of time it took to get approval for a therapy
training project that I proposed. I was supervising graduate students
in psychology, and I had an idea that would enhance the training

experience by providing for observation of the trainees' work. My idea was to put a one-way mirror in the wall between two therapy offices, along with a microphone in one office and a speaker system in the viewing room. A curtain would be installed to cover the one-way mirror when the offices were not being used for observation and training. I priced out the project, which seemed reasonable and well worth the investment. I had used a similar setup in my child therapy practicum at the Vanderbilt Kennedy Center. It took so long to get the hospital administration's approval that I completely forgot about the proposal until I got the green light to proceed.

My administrative supervisor, Ken Stonebraker, was warm and supportive, and we developed a close bond. He respected my work and empowered me to function independently. Ken was older than I was and in a different stage of life as a married man with children, and I felt like a younger brother. We were philosophically compatible in that we both subscribed to a Buddhist approach to life. Ken was without a doubt another angel in my life.

I discovered Joshua Tree National Park, a desert preserve, near the town of 29 Palms, approximately a three-hour drive east of Los Angeles. With traffic it could take four or more hours to get there. Joshua Tree was a timeless, quiet, and surreal landscape, and I considered it to be a sacred place. There was absolutely no ambient city light, so the stars were a brilliant white against the dark sky. I would go on weekends to camp under the stars and experience the peaceful, restorative nature setting. I usually went by myself but on one or two occasions, I went camping at Joshua Tree with Ken.

I also loved the ocean and went for frequent walks in the sand along the shoreline, usually with a stop to sit and meditate. While sitting on one occasion, I noticed another man with a turban meditating in the sand. We struck up a conversation and we traded Indian names.

I told him my Indian name is Sun Dass, which in Hindi translates to "follower of the sun." When he inquired about the name, I said I worship the sun, to which he responded, "Who are you going to thank for the sun?" That got me thinking about where it all comes from. I subsequently read that Pascal, the French philosopher and inventor of the syringe, said, "If you believe in God and he does not exist, you will lose nothing. But if you don't believe in God and he does exist, you will lose everything."

MR found a job in West Los Angeles as an administrative assistant, a position for which she was well suited based on her work history. Our life was joyful and we loved each other, but it became apparent that we were not compatible regarding marriage and children. Accordingly, MR made the painful decision to return to Tennessee, where she reconnected with Tom, a former boyfriend. I mentioned in Chapter 7 that Tom was a wounded Vietnam veteran, paralyzed from the waist down.

After MR left California to return to Tennessee, I sold the VW Beetle with 65,000 miles on it to an eye doctor who wanted a fuel-efficient car for commuting to work, and I replaced it with a 1971 VW Westfalia pop-top camper. Some called this VW model a van or bus, but the unique camper version had a lower double-size bed, an upper bed when the top was raised, an electrical outlet, a clothes closet, and under-bed storage. I added a toilet and a propane tank to power a heater mounted to a lower panel, and additional speakers to the stereo system. Like the 1969 Beetle, the 1971 Westfalia was underpowered. It would slow down to about 50 mph going up hills, but I would compensate by gathering speed going downhill in an effort to keep the vehicle at 60 mph on the uphill grades. It was the perfect RV (recreational vehicle) for my camping trips to Joshua Tree and other beautiful landscapes in California, such as Point Reyes National Seashore,

Redwood National Forest, Sonoma and Napa Valley wineries, Big Sur, and Tassajara Hot Springs. In a citrus-growing area near the town of Ojai, I would always purchase a crate of fresh Valencia oranges. Near Ojai was the Matilija Hot Springs, where I treated myself to my first-ever massage. I remember the massage therapist complimenting my body symmetry, which I attributed to my yoga practice. To face my fear of being alone, I frequently went on these trips alone but sometimes I would invite a girlfriend. In addition to weekend travel, I saved up my vacation time at the hospital and spent four to six weeks during the summers traveling alone in the VW camper.

CHAPTER 9

Solo Van Living

(1975–1976)

IN 1975, AFTER THREE YEARS WORKING at Saint John's Hospital in Santa Monica, I began to feel restless. I had been working fervently for most of my life and I was feeling stressed professionally. I also felt that it was time to fully address my fear of being alone. I was studying the Eastern traditions of Hinduism and Buddhism, and I learned that in India there is a stage of life roughly equivalent to retirement in our country. When the "householder" completes the stages of work and raising a family, he takes a long walk that could last for years. He becomes a wandering sadhu, a monk who the culture supports by providing meals and a place to sleep at virtually any ashram (temple) during the "walk." That appealed to me and I thought, "Why wait until retirement to experience such freedom without responsibilities?" In retrospect, I think I was burning out from post-traumatic stress disorder for so many years. The idea of becoming a wanderer was frightening, and I tried to dismiss it. But it was a persistent thought that seemed to emanate from an inner voice or higher power saying, "You need to do this. Trust it. Go for it."

Before I surrendered to the inner voice advising me to become a wanderer, I had considered other alternatives to practicing psychology. One option, based on my interest and skills as a cook, was to open a vegetarian restaurant in Santa Monica. I imagined a large following of patrons coming to the restaurant for my signature dishes and healthy meals. Perhaps this could be an alternative vehicle for service, for making a difference in the world by introducing people to the idea of food as appetizing *medicine*. I had been studying nutrition by reading and taking workshops on the topic. I studied macrobiotics, vegetarianism, and other diets. I read some of the nutrition classics from the period, such as *Diet for a Small Planet* (1971), and cookbooks such as *Ten Talents* (a cooking guide from the Seventh Day Adventists, 1968), *Laurel's Kitchen: A Handbook for Vegetarian Cookery and Nutrition* (1976), and *The Enchanted Broccoli Forest* (1982).

One culinary learning experience was a weeklong workshop taught by a European nutritionist who had traveled the world to study the diets of people known for health and longevity. I learned that the Hunza, a community of people who live in high-altitude valleys in Pakistan, live long, happy, and hardy lives free of illnesses. Their vegetarian diet consists of a staple of yogurt with raw fruit, nuts, and seeds. They are also active and travel by foot up to two hours from village to farmable land. The Hunza are said to be hardier than the famously strong Sherpa people of the Himalayan region.

I also took a course in tofu-making taught by Bill Shurtleff and Akiko Aoyagi, who wrote *The Book of Tofu: Protein Source of the Future—Now!* (1987). I even made my own soymilk from soybeans, which is the first step in tofu-making. Tofu is essentially the equivalent of cheese but made with soymilk rather than dairy milk.

At one point, I wrote a letter to Ram Dass, an American spiritual teacher, who I considered to be my guru. Ram Dass had been a psychologist who left his teaching position at Harvard University to "practice consciousness full time," as he put it. His departure from Harvard was also a gesture of solidarity with Timothy Leary, a fellow psychologist, who was fired as a result of his experimentation with hallucinogens, notably LSD, and for advocating that people "turn on, tune in, and drop out." I was influenced by Ram Dass's book *Be Here Now* (1970), and had attended some of his lectures. I also had a personal meeting with Ram Dass. In a letter, I asked for his advice on how to handle my identity crisis.

Ram Dass wrote back a short letter, as follows: "I am writing back from aboard a Pan Am flight to India, for God only knows why. *Keep the form of therapist.* It's not so much what role you play in society, but who you are in the role you play." I interpreted this message as meaning I had not made a mistake in becoming a psychologist, and that I should become an *awakened* therapist and teacher. I also interpreted the letter from Ram Dass as support for the idea that what we are called to do can be divinely inspired but may seem irrational.

I finally surrendered to the call to wander, and I made plans to see what it would be like to have no responsibilities, to be truly free. The image that came to mind was a leaf in the wind. I tendered my resignation from my psychologist position at Saint John's Hospital and gave away all my possessions except two things that represented my priorities at the time. I kept my psychologist license in the event I would return to the profession, and I asked Ken Stonebraker to store my stereo system, which included a preamp, a power amp, and a tuner, as well as a pair of large, three-way, bass reflex speakers in walnut cases, all of which I built myself. I set out in January 1975 in the VW camper stocked with provisions and no particular destination or agenda other than to visit a few friends in various parts of the country.

I spent the first night at Bryce Canyon National Park in Arizona and woke up to a stunning blanket of snow adorning the red canyon walls. I was on my way to a friend's house in Logan, Utah, at the foothills of the Wasatch Mountains. Peter was a single graduate student in ornithology—bird study—at Utah State University. He told me he spent most of his time in the library and I was welcome to stay

at his house, in exchange for traveling with him to Mexico to help
gather data for his thesis on bird feeding patterns. I agreed and spent
six weeks at Peter's house experimenting with what it would be like
to have no responsibilities and live with no schedule. I spent my time
reading books, including the *Autobiography of a Yogi* by Paramahansa
Yogananda (1946), *Autobiography of Gandhi* (1927), and the Indian
bible, *Bhagavad Gita*. I also spent time doing yoga, snow-shoeing in
the Wasatch Mountains, and meditating. I ate when I was hungry
and slept when I was tired. What I discovered was that there is no
such thing as nothing. There is always something to be done, even if
it's simply taking care of oneself. Furthermore, I came to understand
that the healthiest way to live is in harmony with nature. No matter
what I did between dawn and dusk, I was sleepy by about nine or ten
in the evening. In retrospect, these insights seem so basic, but at the
time they were revelations.

I left Utah in a caravan with Peter to his bird study site on a private farm in Mexico. He had already obtained permission to camp
on the farm's vast land and study the bird habitat. His thesis focused
on how bird species could predictably be found at different altitudes
depending on the insect and other food supplies available at different
elevations. With binoculars and a tree-height measuring system, we
collected the data for his research. But what is most memorable to me
is how our friendly host Mexican family invited us for dinner each
evening and taught us how to make tortillas from flour and water. It
was a cultural experience in a verdant environment with lush trees
and shrubs.

When Peter and I parted at the end of the expedition to Mexico,
I headed east to visit MR and Tom. My former partner and her hus-
band needed help making the farmhouse they purchased in Franklin,
Tennessee, handicap-accessible. I spent approximately two months

helping them. I slept in my camper while spending the days construct-ing ramps, widening doorways for Tom's wheelchair, and doing other assorted projects.

One interesting project was helping Tom prepare to sell a vintage convertible MG sports car that had been sitting idly in the garage. The car was a beautiful red gem that Tom was unable to drive since he was paralyzed by his Vietnam War injury. His daily driver was a Volvo that was set up with hand controls, and I was amazed that Tom could not only drive the car but also fold up his wheelchair and maneuver it by himself into the area behind the driver's seat. The MG, which was a nostalgic symbol of his pre-Vietnam life, was not equipped for this purpose. We detailed the vehicle and made some mechanical repairs, and I enjoyed driving him around in it until it was sold.

Tom and I connected despite our vastly different Vietnam-era experiences. He was a soldier on the front lines and I was a conscien-tious objector who served in a civilian capacity. I was certainly familiar with trauma and post-traumatic stress disorder, but Tom's traumatic injury was of another magnitude. My relationship with Tom opened my eyes to the life-altering effects of war on surviving soldiers. For example, Tom had some buddies from his time in Vietnam who would visit at the farmhouse. One vet was addicted to alcohol and literally drank a case of beer every day. That is 24 bottles of beer! I cannot drink that much water in a day. I saw how war can wound soldiers not just physically but also emotionally. In fact, I learned that while the U.S. government publishes the number of deaths in war, it rarely, if ever, reports the number of physically injured or emotionally scarred. The number of physically and emotionally wounded warriors almost always exceeds the number of deaths. The term *post-traumatic stress disorder* was coined in relation to Vietnam veterans in the late 1960s, and it is estimated that 25 percent of veterans suffer with this form of anxiety.

While the majority of Vietnam veterans successfully readjusted to postwar life, a substantial number of Vietnam-era veterans have suffered from a variety of psychological and physical injuries. Among the many injuries are symptoms caused by chemical exposure. The U.S. military used more than 19 million gallons of various herbicides, such as Agent Orange, for defoliation and crop destruction in Vietnam. Those who served in Vietnam anytime during the period from 1962 to 1975 are presumed to have been exposed to chemical herbicides. Even short-term exposure to these chemicals, which include dioxin, can cause liver problems, a severe acne-like skin disease called chloracne, type 2 diabetes, immune system dysfunction, nerve disorders, muscular dysfunction, hormone disruption, and heart disease. To me, chemical warfare is simply unconscionable.

PTSD has been recognized by the Veterans Affairs Department as a war injury, and the government agency has led the mental health field in treatment for the disorder. In fact, most of the research on treatment approaches to war-induced trauma, such as prolonged exposure therapy (PE), cognitive behavioral therapy (CBT), eye movement desensitization and reprocessing (EMDR), and medical marijuana is conducted at Veterans Administration hospitals.

Before I left Santa Monica on my solo van pilgrimage, I was in a relationship with a woman named Nancy who I met at Saint John's Hospital. She was the lead interpreter in a mental health program for the deaf. She had fiery blue eyes and long hair, and I nicknamed her "Bluefire." I was amazed at how fast the interpreters could sign during therapy sessions. The two psychologists in the program were not hearing impaired and were not adept at sign language. When they worked with a deaf patient, an interpreter would sit next to them facing the client, verbalize what the patient was communicating in sign language, and use sign language to communicate their verbal responses back to the patient. I learned a little sign language through the relationship and came to appreciate this amazing skill. Nancy took a leave of absence to visit me in Tennessee and to decide whether to join me on the road with no destination. After a few weeks she decided to return to her job at the hospital. We kept in touch, but I was alone once again.

CHAPTER 10

Venice, California

(1976–1977)

AFTER ALMOST A YEAR living and traveling in the camper van, I began to realize that psychology was my connection to other people as well as my purpose in life. I saw that doing therapy and sharing with others what I had learned about dealing with anxiety was what I was put here to do. I understood that what happens to us is one thing, and how we choose to use what happens to us is another thing. I could integrate and use my trauma-recovery experiences to make a difference in the world. I decided to return to California and seek an opportunity to work again as a psychologist.

Two miracles occurred when I returned to California. First, the chief psychologist at Saint John's Hospital in Santa Monica—Joan Madsen—invited me back to work in my previous position in the mental health program. She explained that another psychologist in the program was retiring, leaving an opening if I was interested. The only caveat was that I had to agree to stay at least two years, which, after being homeless for a year, I gladly agreed to do. Unbelievably, I was back in the very same office I left the year before, and for the first few months I felt like I had a dream in which I quit my job and went on a pilgrimage in a VW camper van.

On my return to Santa Monica, I rented a furnished house in the Pacific Palisades, an upscale community in Los Angeles County. It was comfortable but lonely, and I knew it was time for me to develop new friendships and social connections. I decided to relocate, and I rented a large, three-bedroom house available from one of the psychologists I knew from the deaf mental health program. My intention was to open it up to housemates and establish a communal living arrangement with some like-minded people. The house was in Venice, just steps from the beach where I often went to swim and meditate when I lived in Santa Monica. I posted a "Seeking Housemates" notice at the local health food store. Shortly thereafter, I received a call from a woman representing two couples who were looking for a place to live. The four people consisted of a married couple, Barry and Moira, and each of their sisters, who were in a relationship with each other. It seemed a bit unusual, but it looked like a good fit for the two empty bedrooms. When they came to visit the house, we made an instant connection and agreed they would move in.

It was an adventurous experiment that worked out well. In fact, Barry became a close friend for the next 35 years, and he served as another angel in my life. We both ended up in Vermont, where he had previously lived and worked as a ski mechanic. At the risk of jumping ahead in this book to my move to Vermont, Barry taught me how to ski and we skied at Stowe Mountain Resort, Smugglers' Notch, and Sugarbush Resort. Barry was the most graceful skier I have ever seen in more than 30 years of skiing. We looked like synchronized skiers gracefully bombing down the mountains.

Unfortunately, I had a traumatic experience while living in Venice. One night, as I was sleeping on my futon, I heard a noise in the kitchen that sounded like a drawer closing shut. I fell back asleep but I was awakened again by an intruder in my bedroom. It was dark and I could not see clearly, but a male voice said sternly, "Don't move or I'll shoot!" I knew in that moment that it was important to keep my cool and, using my natural people skills and psychology training,

I asked him who he was, what was he doing there, and what he wanted. In response, he repeated, "Don't move or I'll shoot!" Keeping in mind that my bed was a futon mattress on the floor, I slowly grasped my pillow, jumped up, and swung the pillow at the intruder. I then grabbed his arm to dislodge his weapon, which turned out to be a kitchen knife he had taken from the drawer that I heard closing before he entered my room. As he dropped the knife, he started to plead for me for to let him go. I held on as he backed out of the bedroom where a hallway sconce revealed that he was a frightened teenager begging to be released. In a moment of compassion, I let him go and he ran out the entrance door. I then fell apart thinking about what could have gone wrong. It turned out that one of the sisters had gone out to pick up her partner from an evening job and left the door unlocked. The would-be robber must have assumed no one was home. I had no training in self-defense, but I believe my meditation and yoga practice helped me stay focused and in control of myself in the face of threat.

The second miracle that occurred after returning to Santa Monica was meeting Sheryl, an athletic and attractive medical social worker who worked at the same hospital. Sheryl and I found ourselves talking and getting to know each other, and I learned that she also grew up in New York City. It was not long before we made plans to have dinner together. She invited me to her garden apartment on San Vicente Boulevard, a main avenue near the ocean that was lined with tall palm trees. As I entered her apartment, I noticed a bicycle and a pair of skis on her balcony. This excited me, and I thought to myself, "This is a yet another sign of compatibility!" And it was. We came from similar backgrounds and we liked some of the same outdoor recreational activities. Like me, she was also a vegetarian. Sheryl made a memorable Mexican dinner that was followed by a magical night together. At a later point in time, Sheryl revealed that after our very first meeting she told her supervisor, "I just met the man I'm going to marry!"

I have had many "angel relationships" in my life, but there was a special depth with Sheryl that made me feel I had met my soul mate. Despite my trauma history, I never gave up on love. I believed in soul mate relationships and the idea that someday I would meet a person with whom I was meant to be. I was, to put it simply, a romantic who believed that the Cinderella story was a metaphor for what can happen in real life. Something happened to me when I met Sheryl, and I found myself thinking of her constantly, writing love notes and placing them on the windshield of her car, and looking forward to the next time I would see her.

Many people wonder how they will know they are in love. One of my psychology interns shared an interaction he had with an adult client. He told me that he asked her if she loved her children, to which she replied without hesitation, "Of course I love my children." He then asked, "How do you know that you love your children?" She seemed surprised and responded, "I just know!" I think that is the answer to the perennial question. Falling in love cannot be understood by rational thinking. Love happens at a deep and intuitive level that is experienced as "just knowing."

On the other hand, as I have pointed out elsewhere, trauma victims tend to distrust their feelings, intuition, and judgment. Distinguishing between a wish and an intuition can be confusing. Love is too great a risk for those who have been hurt or betrayed, especially by people they trusted.

Furthermore, it can be difficult to separate lust from love, physical attraction from emotional compatibility. Victims of sexual abuse may believe their value lies in their sexuality, and may become promiscuous in the search for love, emotional connection, and validation. In other cases, sexual abuse victims may become inhibited and sexually repressed as a coping mechanism for having being violated.

In the Jewish tradition, it is believed that at the moment each person is born there is another person, already born or yet to be born, who is a matching soul mate. From this perspective, one of our purposes in life is to find that matching soul. When I met and got to know Sheryl, I felt I had met my matching soul.

As I mentioned in Chapter 1, I grew up playing guitar, though I was inconsistent and stopped altogether in graduate school. But music was always an important part of my life, as it has been for so many people throughout history. I have a T-shirt from the Musical Instrument Museum that I purchased when I visited Scottsdale, Arizona, on a speaking trip. The T-shirt reads in six different languages, "Music is the language of the soul." When I started playing again in 2012, after a hiatus of 35 years, I also began to write music and songs. One of my songs is about soul mates. Entitled "Soul Love," here are the lyrics to the song:

Soul Love
Paul Foxman

VERSE 1

I think about you baby
Every day and every night
When you put your arms around me
It always feels so right

CHORUS

That's why my soul is incomplete without your love

VERSE 2

I want and need you baby
And I know you feel it too
When you tell me that you love me
You always say it like it's true

CHORUS

BRIDGE /REFRAIN

I knew that it was possible to meet someone like you
An angel sent to me from high above
My heart is full and all my dreams with you they will come true
That's why my soul is incomplete without your love

VERSE 3

I see you reaching for me
You're calling out my name
Since you opened to me baby
I will never be the same

CHORUS

VERSE 4

Our connection is magnetic
We are mirrors of each other
You fulfill all my desires
I will never need another

CHORUS (2x)

That's why my soul is now complete with your sweet love

I organized a dance party at the Venice house and proudly introduced Sheryl to my new California friends. Sheryl and I had become a couple and we decided to live together. We rented a stucco cottage with a tiled roof on the property of a Mexican hacienda in the heart of Santa Monica. The eccentric owner, who lived in the main house, would rent the cottages only to vegetarians, and we were required to have a personal interview. I will never forget the owner saying during the interview, "You have to watch out for meat-eaters . . . they *kill*!" We lived there for two wonderful years.

One night as we were sleeping, I had a vivid dream that seemed like more than a dream. I heard a girl's voice circling around my head asking, "When do I get to come in? When do I get to come in?" In the morning, I told Sheryl about the dream and, amazingly, she had the *same dream* that night. This simultaneous dream convinced us that the voice was real, that this was not an auditory hallucination. We concluded that a girl spirit visited us and asked us to be her parents and bring her into the physical world. Approximately two years later, after we married, we had our first child . . . a girl! We believe our first daughter, Kali Dawn, was the girl spirit who visited us in that dream to let us know we were chosen to be her parents.

When Sheryl and I decided to marry and have children, we thought it would make sense to move back east to be closer to our families. We believed we would benefit from family support, including help raising children. We gave our resignation notices from our jobs at Saint John's Hospital, put some possessions in storage, and left for a drive across the country in the VW camper.

Sheryl was a runner and a swimmer. As a runner she would train up to 14 miles a day and she ran in the famed Santa Monica Marathon, placing high enough in her age group to win a medal. This was just another sign of compatibility considering my history as a runner, my role as captain of my high school track team, and training at Yale under the guidance of the 1964 U.S. Olympic track and field coach. As a swimmer, Sheryl had also worked as a lifeguard at a pool in Brooklyn. On the drive heading east, she proposed that whenever we came across a lake she would go for a swim. In addition, when we came to a long downhill she would get out for a run while I followed in the van. I remember her first swim on the trip. It was at Lake Havasu in Arizona, a large man-made lake resulting from the construction in 1938 of the Parker Dam on the Colorado River near the border of Arizona and California. Lake Havasu is actually a large reservoir spanning more than 19,000 acres with 450 miles of shoreline. The average depth of the water is 35 feet and in some parts of the lake it is 90 feet deep. In 1980, when we stopped to visit Lake Havasu, the water was crystal clear and we could see straight through to the bottom. I thought Sheryl would simply go for a short swim to refresh herself, but as I watched from shore, I was blown away at how long she could swim. I watched her swim gracefully for at least an hour and thought, "This woman was born in water!" Her road runs were equally long and I was happy to accommodate since we were under no time pressure.

I was happy to practice yoga as my exercise as well as ride my bicycle. My running days had come to an end as a result of a running injury that derailed me. The injury was to my right hip and was attributable to the wall-mounted track in my high school gymnasium. The track had a steeply banked side wall with a cork surface, and because we trained in the usual counterclockwise direction, my right leg could not fully extend on the turns. As my right leg repeatedly pounded the sidewall, shocking my hip, I developed a vexatious hip injury that hurts when I run.

Although we planned to be closer to our families, Sheryl and I did not want to return to New York City. On a map of the northeast, I used a compass to draw a circle representing a 400-mile radius—a one-day drive—from New York City. We wanted a rural but cultured place to live if we could find it. We planned to explore within the 400-mile radius that included Connecticut, Massachusetts, New Hampshire, Vermont, Upstate New York, Pennsylvania, New Jersey, Delaware, and northern Virginia. We almost settled in Charlottesville, Virginia, a college town nestled in the Blue Ridge Mountains and close enough to Virginia Beach for a day trip to the ocean. The four-season climate seemed to be hospitable. There was even a ski mountain—Winter-green Resort—only 26 miles from town. Charlottesville appeared to match our criteria.

CHAPTER 11

Bennington, Vermont

(1980–1983)

BEFORE COMMITTING TO CHARLOTTESVILLE, Sheryl and I took some advice from Barry, our friend from Santa Monica, who insisted that we check out Vermont before making a decision as to where we would settle. Barry had lived for 10 years in the Waitsfield Valley near Burlington, where he went to Goddard College, worked as a ski mechanic, and skied at Mount Ellen, now known as Sugarbush Resort. On the way, we explored western Massachusetts and entered Vermont through the town of Brattleboro on Route 91, one of only two interstate highways in the state. We suddenly understood why Vermont is known as the Green Mountain State. The color of the rich forested foliage was greener than I had ever seen, including North Carolina's Blue Ridge Mountains, Tennessee's Great Smoky Mountains, and New York's Adirondack Mountains. We felt a strong connection to nature, and did not realize at first that there are no billboards allowed on Vermont roadways. The state's primary industry is tourism, and the Vermont "brand" is all about natural.

We visited Burlington, a college town located between the Green Mountains and 110-mile-long Lake Champlain. Burlington, like Charlottesville, is a college town rich in culture. There are actually five colleges in the Burlington area, as well as the restored Flynn Theatre that draws national talent, the Contois Auditorium for music concerts, and the annual Vermont City Marathon that became a qualifying event for the New York and Boston marathons. There was also an annual outdoor jazz festival. And the politics were compatible: When we visited in 1980, Vermont had a Jewish woman governor, Madeleine Kunin, and the mayor of Burlington was Bernie Sanders, a popular progressive mayor who served for four terms. In addition to Burlington's culture, Vermont offered unlimited opportunities for outdoor recreation that included our favorite activities such as skiing, hiking, kayaking, and bike riding. As we sat in the sand on the Burlington Bay waterfront, we were reminded of the ocean in Santa Monica and we concluded that this could be our new home state. Barry often referred to Lake Champlain as the "west coast of New England."

On our mission to discover where to settle and have a family, we stopped to visit one of Sheryl's cousins in Manhattan. She lived in an upscale apartment on the West Side, adjacent to Riverside Park. We visited for less than an hour and left to find that the VW camper had been burglarized. The vehicle was completely cleaned out and we lost everything of value, including my backpack with my camera and binoculars. Even the stereo was removed from the dashboard. The only thing not missing was Sheryl's jewelry, which she had cleverly stored in a cloth case she had made and hid under the camper mattress. The police, to whom we reported the burglary, told us a camper with California plates and curtains would be a "sitting duck" for a burglary. Once again, I was reminded of my traumatic childhood in New York City, where danger lurks around every corner, even in ritzy neighborhoods.

Sheryl and I had been unemployed for several months during our journey to find a home. As we were planning our wedding, we felt some pressure to find work. I reached out to the University of Vermont's department of psychology, as well as to some private practices, but found no openings. We expanded our search and I found a job as the director of adult outpatient services at a mental health center in Bennington, Vermont, about three hours south of Burlington and not far from Albany, New York. My start date was just a week after our wedding in September 1980.

Our wedding was a do-it-yourself event that took place outdoors in Spring Valley, New York, in the backyard of my brother, Eric's, house. Sheryl and I handled all the details, which included a tent with vegetarian food, recorded music, and a rabbi who would marry a Jewish woman and a not-so-Jewish Buddhist-aligned man. Our families attended, along with a few friends, for a total of about 40 people. We hid some speakers in the trees and our wedding processional was accompanied by music from the English rock group Supertramp emanating from the trees. As a statement of our values, we ordered a cream-frosted carrot cake for the wedding. We had a short honeymoon at Lake Sunapee, New Hampshire, where we stayed at the Follansbee Inn, spending considerable time on the phone negotiating an offer we made on a house in Arlington, Vermont, near enough to my new job in Bennington.

We ended up purchasing our very first house in Old Bennington, close enough for me to walk to work. It was the caretaker's home adjacent to a Victorian mansion that had fallen into disrepair. The house was 120 years old and, believe it or not, it was never insulated. We had to eat in the living room, near the Vermont Castings wood stove. I started remodeling the house almost immediately, replacing window trim, repointing the chimney, and painting the kitchen cabinets. In the time period in which the house was built, people used armoires for their clothes, so there were virtually no closets in the house. Accordingly, I built closets, including wiring them for lights. We installed new landscaping and I painted the outside of the house.

Three years later, when we relocated to Burlington and sold the Bennington house, we were rewarded for our efforts with a significant equity jump.

United Counseling Service in Bennington was the agency that hired me to direct the adult outpatient program. I was responsible for six or seven therapists, as well as a 24-hour emergency service. It was a significant adjustment as I had little management experience except for the tribe director position at the summer camp in Quebec and the supervisor job at the residential treatment center in Florida. The director position had been unfilled for a year before I took the job and the professional staff were unaccustomed to having a boss. I quickly learned that being a leader is not a popularity contest. It is not about being *liked* but rather about being *respected*. What worked for me as a leader was establishing credibility through fairness, transparency, and authenticity. I won over the staff and was asked by the executive director of the agency to open a branch office in Manchester, an upscale community about 30 minutes north of Bennington. The experiment was to see whether I could create a profitable outpatient practice that did not depend on grants. I rented a suite of offices, furnished the space, and hired some therapists as well as an office manager.

The branch office proved to be a moneymaker while providing quality services under my supervision. This experience gave me the confidence to pursue my dream of a private practice in Burlington, Vermont. The incentive to start a practice in Burlington was based not only on our positive feelings about that community, but also on how little culture there was in Bennington. For example, there was no gym in town, no theater, no concert venues, and we had to drive 45 minutes over to Albany, New York, to shop for virtually everything other than food.

Sheryl and I had our first child, Kali, in 1982, while living in Bennington. Actually, she was born in Pittsfield, Massachusetts, at a birth center about 45 minutes across the state line that provided for home-style births. How ironic that we could walk to the local hospital but we could not find an obstetrician or other medical backup for a home birth. There is no doubt that Kali is the girl whose voice came to us in that simultaneous dream several years earlier in Santa Monica. We are so happy she waited for us to bring her into the world. I actually delivered her at the birth center and cut her umbilical cord before handing her over to Sheryl. Childbirth is nothing short of a miracle, and I believe that if all fathers participated in the birth of their children, there would be less abuse and domestic violence.

While living and working in Bennington, I added a part-time job teaching at Antioch New England College in Keene, New Hampshire, a 45-minute drive over the Green Mountains. I taught in the master's program in counseling psychology, designed primarily for second-career adults. My responsibilities included a course called the professional seminar, which involved managing the counseling internships of my students in various settings in New England. Once per year, I would travel to evaluate the internship settings and meet with each of my students' supervisors. This responsibility led to a fortuitous meeting with two psychologists at a private practice in the Burlington area. Marc and Judith Mann were the psychologists-owners at Family Therapy Associates, where one of my students was interning. The meeting was warm and friendly, and we made a strong connection. During the meeting, I learned that the practice did not have a child psychologist on staff. Shortly after the visit, I contacted the Manns to express interest in joining the group to complement their services with my child therapy experience. We visited again and mutually decided to make it happen.

To join a private practice in the Burlington area would require me to resign from my job at United Counseling Service, the mental health center in Bennington. It would also mean that to honor my teaching commitment at Antioch New England in Keene, New Hampshire, I would have to drive three hours each way once a week. To make the transition gradually, I arranged to use my vacation time at the mental health center to begin seeing patients in the private practice. It was a three-hour drive between the two settings, and I began with one day per week in private practice, spending the night in my camper and driving back to the mental health center at the end of the workday. I knew that when my schedule reached two full days in practice I would need to resign from the mental health center. It would take a leap of faith to leave the security of a salaried job for a private practice with no guaranties of sustainability. But my heart was set on being my own boss, and I soon tendered my resignation in Bennington.

When I informed the executive director at the mental health center of my decision to leave, she asked me to reconsider. A day later, she called me and said, "I have been empowered by the board of directors to give you whatever it takes to keep you here." I paused briefly at the attractive offer and did a quick cost-benefit analysis of the finances. Despite the security of the salaried position at the mental health center, my heart was in private practice, so I declined the offer and began to make plans to relocate to the Burlington area with Sheryl and our one-year-old daughter. There were multiple risks involved in that decision. First, there is no guarantee that in private practice there will be enough referrals to make an adequate living. Second, we would need to find housing in the new location with no guarantee that we would be able to sell our house in Bennington. And furthermore, we had the responsibility of providing security for our young child. On the surface, it seemed like an irrational plan, but my deeper intuition told me it was the right thing to do.

Trauma makes it difficult for us to trust our intuition and follow our hearts, especially when it takes us out of our comfort zones. Many decisions in life require intuition as much as rational thinking. The main job of our brains is to keep us alive, and our survival instinct prefers predictability, sameness, and as little risk-taking as possible. Ambiguity, uncertainty, and unpredictability are threats to our survival instinct and raise anxiety regarding change. Many people with anxiety, particularly trauma-related anxiety, do not like change and tend to hold back or avoid pursuing their dreams when there is no guarantee of a positive outcome. This was what I had to deal with whenever I was faced with making big decisions, such as whether to move from San Francisco to Nashville in order to obtain a PhD in psychology, or when I made the decision to take off in a VW camper for an undefined length of time to face my fears of being alone. For others, starting a business, changing jobs, leaving an abusive relationship, or travel might evoke anxiety and lead to playing it safe and then regretting it.

Going on trust and faith, we made a commitment to buy a house in Essex, near the practice I was joining, on the hope that our Bennington house would sell in time to close on the new property. The market was quiet and there was not a single offer on our Bennington house for several months, during which the closing on the new house was approaching. The risk was that we would be saddled with two mortgages as winter set in when the housing market in Vermont tends to go into hibernation. Then one day, when I came home from work at the mental health center, I learned that there were two full-price offers on the house. Each party knew they were competing against another interested party. The real estate agent came to our house with the two offers in hand. One offer was from an attorney in New Jersey who drove up to Vermont with his wife and daughter in a red Porsche. They videotaped the house without our permission and planned to use the house as a second home, knowing there were ski resorts nearby, as well as the famous Battenkill River for fishing and water sports. Sheryl, who was home at the time of their visit, told me they were arrogant and insensitive and she did not want to sell our house to them. However, they made a full-price cash offer with no contingencies. This would normally be considered the ideal buyer.

The other party was a young couple with two young daughters who were moving to Bennington from Burlington. That would be coincidence enough but, in addition, they loved the house and Sheryl liked them. However, their offer included a financing contingency as well as a need to sell their house in Burlington in order to proceed with purchasing our house. The realtor put the two offers on our kitchen table and said, "This is a no-brainer. You should accept the cash offer from the New Jersey couple." We went against our intuition and took the realtor's advice.

As it turned out, the New Jersey couple did not show for the closing on our Bennington house. They simply disappeared with no notice or communication. The fact that they lost a $2,000 deposit was not much consolation as we faced the prospect of having to manage the mortgage payments on two houses. Moreover, we lost at least two months of time during which we had taken the Bennington house off the market. My heart sank and my anxiety escalated.

I decided to take matters into my own hands and I called the couple in Burlington to see if they were still looking for a house in Bennington. Miraculously, they had not yet found a house and they were delighted to hear from me. We made the deal without the realtors, although they did get their commissions. Once we had the real estate issue resolved, we started packing for the relocation to Essex, Vermont. What I took from this experience is that intuition is as important as reason, if not more so. I think we need both heart and mind to navigate successfully through life.

CHAPTER 12

Essex, Vermont

(1983–1985)

FAMILY THERAPY ASSOCIATES, the psychology practice I was joining, was located in the town of Essex Junction, Vermont. In 1983, Essex Junction was home to an IBM plant, which was the second-largest employer in Vermont, second only to the Vermont state government. IBM had 9,000 employees working three shifts and the plant was within walking distance from the psychology practice. I predicted correctly that many of my patients would be IBM employees, such as engineers, chemists, production technicians, secretaries, and managers, as well as their children. Indeed, it did not take long before my caseload was full. My practice saw the full range of presenting problems, including anxiety, depression, eating disorders, marital problems, divorce adjustment, midlife crises, gender identity issues, and addictions. There were eight other therapists including Sheryl, who joined as a licensed psychologist with a half-time schedule balanced with parenting our children.

The home we purchased was a large, 10-year-old split-level house with three bedrooms, one and a half bathrooms, and a two-car underground garage on Chapin Road in the town of Essex (not to be confused with Essex Junction). It was a step up from the small, uninsulated house we lived in for three years in Bennington. The house was on 10 acres of land with a long, gravel driveway, across the road from an apple orchard, not surprisingly named Chapin Orchard.

I started remodeling on the very first night we moved in. I started with the kitchen where a row of cabinets over an island were much too low, resulting in a passageway between the kitchen and dining room that required bending over to see through. I remember jumping up from the dinner table and pulling the cabinets from the kitchen ceiling, exposing the wiring that provided lighting on the underside of the cabinets. It looked like a tornado had hit the house. We proceeded to install a new counter and replace the hardware on the remaining kitchen cabinets. Not long after the kitchen renovation, I modified a wall between the kitchen and living room to create a more contemporary open floor plan. I moved on to divide a large bedroom into a still-sizable bedroom and a second bathroom.

The house had vinyl siding in a hideous green color and, after some research, I learned that vinyl siding can be painted if it is sufficiently oxidized. At 10 years old, the vinyl siding was, indeed, oxidized, and I painted the entire outside with a wood-tone paint using a roller. All the skills I had acquired in my summer jobs during college at Yale—electrical, plumbing, carpentry, Sheetrock, and painting—came into good use. I also added a new skill, the art of wallpapering.

We had our second daughter in the Essex house. It was a true home birth that took place in our bedroom. She was born as the sun was setting and we named her Leah Sunset, in keeping with the name of our first daughter, Kali Dawn, who was born at the break of day two years earlier.

As we began to look ahead at raising two children, we focused on where they would go to school. We were interested in the Waldorf approach to education, to which I was exposed through my brother, Eric, who went to the Rudolf Steiner School in Manhattan. Steiner was a renaissance man who was hired to establish a school for the children of workers at the Waldorf-Astoria cigarette factory in Stuttgart,

Germany. The Waldorf school philosophy centers on the idea of preserving childhood by pacing learning with the development of the human brain. Speaking generally, the curriculum is designed to mirror the history of man, starting with the oral tradition of storytelling, leading to drawing (pictographs)—which were the earliest forms of writing—and, finally, to reading. It takes four to five years for the reading curriculum to catch up to the typical public-school curriculum, and the educational approach is believed to be more in sync with the developing brain. The movement has morphed into the largest private school system in the world with some 400 Waldorf schools, including approximately 90 in the United States.

We met some other people with young families who were considering options for educating their children. We formed a study group that met weekly and rotated the meeting location among our homes. We met for two years before we committed to a parent-run Waldorf school, at which point we rented space in a church in Shelburne, Vermont, hired our first kindergarten teacher, and named it the Lake Champlain Waldorf School. Our daughter, Kali, was in the lead class.

A series of miracles occurred once we made a commitment to start the Lake Champlain Waldorf School. One was a gift of wooded land in Shelburne on which we could build our school. The land was donated by one of the founding families. We were also able to obtain a building loan from the Association of Waldorf Schools of North America, as well as guidance and consultation from that organization. I recall weekend work sessions during which we poured concrete for a floor with radiant heat to keep the children warm through Vermont's cold winters. One of the parents was a contractor who donated his time and expertise to the project. We were part of a beautiful community of people with shared values and visions. It was a magical process, and the school grew over the years during which a second location was established for the Lake Champlain Waldorf High School. This successful undertaking is one of the accomplishments, or triumphs, of which I am most proud. When my time comes to leave this world, I will leave behind this contribution and lasting legacy.

When we felt we had completed our role in creating the Lake Champlain Waldorf School, Sheryl and I decided to move to the country. We sold the Essex house and purchased a farmhouse in Jeffersonville at the foothills of the Smugglers' Notch ski resort. The following chapter recounts the trials and tribulations of this adventure.

CHAPTER 13

Jeffersonville, Vermont

(1986–1987)

JEFFERSONVILLE IS A RURAL COMMUNITY approximately 25 miles north of Essex, and another 7 miles from Burlington. The drive itself is scenic, especially along Pleasant Valley Road from Underhill to Jeffersonville, which winds through farmland at the foothills of the Green Mountains. The plan was to commute to our offices in Essex Junction, a decision that turned out to be more stressful than we anticipated. The farmhouse we purchased in Jeffersonville was once part of a large farm whose owners parceled off 10 acres with the original farmhouse and outbuildings; as a retirement plan, they built a modern house with nice views on the larger property. Our property included a 40-stall cow barn and a carriage house, and it had a direct view southeast to the ski trails at Smugglers' Notch Resort. There were wide-board pine floors on the second level and I noted a hardwood maple floor through a hole in the linoleum of the kitchen-dining area. The house had real potential and, on a handshake, a local banker signed off on a bridge loan that would enable us to remodel the house until our Essex house was sold.

We hired a contractor to help us remodel the Jefferson farmhouse. We gutted most of the house, which had lath and plaster walls. Anyone who has ever gutted a lath and plaster wall knows how messy the job can be, as it involves breaking down the plaster with a sledgehammer and pulling off the lath to get to the studs. We called a trash company and ordered a construction bin; when they rolled the giant bin off the truck, we thought we could never fill it. As it turned out, with the construction debris consisting of plaster, lath, old wiring, rotting wood, linoleum flooring, and old kitchen cabinets, along with trash we found on the property, we filled the bin to the brim. Among the many changes we made was removing the dark and dreary front porch to bring sunlight into the house. We replaced the dining room door to the porch with a huge picture window with a direct view of the ski resort. With binoculars, you could see the ski trails on Morse, Sterling, and Madonna Mountains.

The house remodel was a major project and I took a considerable number of days off from work to manage the job. At one point, as we were in the final phase of the remodel, the contractor disappeared with his crew. My theory is they did not want to tackle one of the dustiest jobs of the project: sanding the maple and pine floors. Fortunately, I had experience with drum sanding machines and I proceeded to sand and refinish the floors. Since we had written and signed work orders with the contractor, we were able to sue him for breach of contract. We prevailed, but it was small consolation for being left to finish the job ourselves. In the end, with a new entrance, new kitchen and bathroom, skylights in the second-floor bedrooms, shining wood floors, and picturesque location, it was a magazine-worthy country home. We named the property "Winterhill."

There were several rewards for the blood, sweat, and tears we put into moving to Jeffersonville and remodeling the farmhouse. Living at the foot of a ski resort made it possible for me to take our two young girls skiing twice per week to free Sheryl up to study for her psychology license exam. Whereas I obtained my Vermont psychology license in 1980, on a reciprocity basis with my active licenses in Tennessee and California, Sheryl was not yet licensed as a psychologist. She has a master's degree in counseling psychology, which qualifies her for Vermont's unique option of licensing psychologists at the master's level as distinct from doctoral. Vermont is one of only two states in the U.S. that provides for licensing of master's-level psychologists, the other being West Virginia. The history behind this option is that as a rural state with a shortage of health care providers, Vermont could meet the need for mental health services by opening up to psychologists and psychotherapists with a master's degree rather than restrict licensure to doctoral-level psychologists. There simply were not enough doctoral psychologists in the state. For a few months after we finished the house, Sheryl and I made the following agreement: On two days every week, I would take our girls, who were just short of five and three years old, to the Smugglers' Notch children's nursery and introduce them to skiing. This would give Sheryl time to focus on studying for her licensing exam, which I am proud to say she passed on the first try. It is common for psychologists to fail on the first or even second try.

I took the girls out on the beginner slopes one at a time and taught them how to ski. I used the "Bert and Ernie method": I put a Bert sticker on one ski and an Ernie sticker on the other ski. I also used two small C-clamps and a section of rubber tubing to connect the tips of the two skis together. This resulted in a permanent but flexible snowplow position, and they learned to turn by alternately putting weight on the Bert or Ernie ski as I directed. I did my best to make it fun by keeping the ski lessons brief and packing appealing lunches and buying them hot chocolate drinks. The investment paid off as Leah, our younger daughter, competed on the Nordic ski team in high school. And I remember Kali, our older daughter, as a young adult, teaching a boyfriend how to ski.

Another benefit of the Jeffersonville phase of my life is that I became involved as a psychologist in the Lamoille County school systems. I earned the respect of several rural school systems in Jeffersonville, Johnson, Hyde Park, Fletcher, and Eden that hired me regularly to evaluate students whose emotional, behavioral, or intellectual challenges were impacting their academic progress. This became a niche in my private practice that lasted for many years.

While we lived in Jeffersonville, Barry and Moira, our friends from Santa Monica, returned to Vermont and bought a house nearby in the town of Belvidere. This enabled us to spend time together, especially enjoying skiing at Smugglers' Notch. As I noted previously, Barry was an angel in my life and, as an expert skier, and he was more than happy to mentor me in the sport. I remember the very first time I rented ski equipment and went out on the mountain with Barry. As an athletic person, skiing came naturally to me and I was quickly hooked. The very next day I showed up at the Downhill Edge ski shop in Burlington and purchased my first set of ski equipment. Years later, I became a ski instructor as a weekend job at another ski resort, Sugarbush, which enabled me to ski without paying for ski tickets that are now in the range of $100 per day. For each day that I taught skiing, I would receive a day pass to be used at any time. Barry and I skied together often and engaged in sangha conversations on the ski lift. I credit our conversations with the inspiration for my first book, *Dancing With Fear*, originally published in 1994.

A few years later, my love for skiing inspired a ski trip to France with Sheryl. We stayed at a quaint hotel in Megève, a town in the Chamonix Valley. Whereas we have mountains in the U.S., the Alps in France are mountain *ranges*, where you can ski from one town to another through a series of lifts and downhill descents. The highlight of the trip was a day skiing down a 20 kilometer couloir, a glacial ski run starting from a peak known as L'Aiguille du Midi (Eye of the Midday), which is more than 3,000 feet above sea level. It takes all day to make the run down the glacier, with a lunch stop at a restaurant accessible only by a ski lift.

Despite the multiple benefits of living in Jeffersonville, there was one insurmountable problem with living in the country. As Jeffersonville was 25 miles from our offices in Essex Junction, and another 7 miles to the city of Burlington, we were spending too much time in the car and not enough time enjoying the house. With traffic, it could take an hour to go shopping for anything other than food, and the nearest health food store was in Burlington. We realized that we made a premature back-to-the-land move that would have been better timed as a retirement plan. Within a few months of moving into the remodeled Jeffersonville house, we had to accept that it was not working for us. But how would we transition back to "civilization"?

We were concerned that we would not be able to recoup our investment in the Jeffersonville house in such a short period of time. The majority of potential buyers would be more attracted to the Burlington area, where some of the school systems were known to be excellent, and goods and services would be just minutes away. We were certain we would take a loss. But I had an insight that saved us from a financial disaster. I thought if we subdivided the 10 acres into a section that included the house, and a second parcel that included some open land with a 40-stall cow barn, we could increase the value of the property. We could conceivably sell the property to two buyers, or command a higher price for the combined two lots. We hired a surveyor to mark off the two parcels and registered them with the town. The idea worked. We sold the entire property to a couple from Boston who were looking for a home that would accommodate their horses. It was a perfect solution.

Once we had a buyer for the Jeffersonville house, we contracted to build a house in Williston, a historic town located within 20 minutes of the heart of Burlington. The school system, which we checked out carefully, was excellent. In fact, the principal of the kindergarten through middle school was a former Montessori schoolteacher who was familiar with the Waldorf philosophy.

At the closing of the sale of the Jeffersonville property, I was monitoring the banker's math and noticed that the numbers were not adding up. In the parking lot after the closing, I realized the bank had incorrectly given us a check for $20,000 more than we were entitled to receive. The bank had made a $20,000 mistake. Our attorney suggested that just for fun, we immediately deposit the check in our bank account, after which Sheryl and I went out to dinner to celebrate the sale of the house. When we returned to the house, there was a note on the front door. The bank had sent several officers to let us know they made a mistake, and asked that we call the bank as soon as possible in the morning. We called the bank and played dumb, knowing of course that we would need to refund the extra money.

Having closed on the sale, we began packing for our move to Williston, where our new house was built in an astounding 13 weeks, coinciding with the closing on the Jeffersonville house.

CHAPTER 14

Williston, Vermont

(1987–2012)

We chose to make Williston our new community, primarily based on its historic, small-town feeling as well as excellent school system. Similar to the Waldorf philosophy of education, the the kindergarten through eighth grade Williston Central School, organizes students into multigrade groups called "families of learners." Each family has its own physical location, called a "house," with core teachers, referred to as "facilitators." Students remain with their house and facilitators for four years, which provides time to develop relationships with peers and teachers. In the Waldorf approach, students stay with the same teacher for eight years based on the same principles. The learning environment at Williston Central School is open and flexible, with partitioned areas for different learning activities as well as teachers' offices.

Like the Waldorf school system, there are no number grades at all during the eight years that students attend Williston Central School. Instead of grades, which rate a student's learning progress in relation to other students, a rubric system is used to evaluate learning progress two times each year. Assessment of each student's academic progress is based on the Vermont Department of Education's learning goals for each year in each subject. For example, a fifth-grade student could be rated as 75 percent toward the learning goals in fifth-grade math, or a third-grade student could be rated as 50 percent toward the learning goal in third-grade reading. Students are asked to attend the parent-teacher progress reviews, and they are given a voice in the discussion.

Each house includes a quiet, carpeted area with open seating, called a "kiva," named for its similarity to the underground meditation rooms used in some Native American adolescent rites of passage. The kiva is the central meeting place for the house, and it also serves as the venue for students' presentations to peers and facilitators. All students are encouraged to demonstrate the results of learning projects in the form of presentations to their school family. Parents are encouraged to attend the kiva presentations, which can range from conventional talks with posters and flip charts to music videos and computer-animated shows, all followed by questions and feedback from peers, facilitators, and parents. This is an excellent example of how to incorporate some of the most important life skills into the elementary and middle school curriculum. The opportunity to practice such skills at a young age can also go a long way toward preventing anxiety associated with public speaking—one of the most common phobias.

Keeping in mind my interest and commitment to education, as well as my role in creating the Lake Champlain Waldorf School, Williston Central School's approach to education was compatible with my values and beliefs. These values can be summed up in Williston Central School's mission statement:

> We believe that each individual, regardless of age or experience, is capable of learning and that every learner can master the behaviors, skills, and knowledge essential for a contributing member of a democratic society. The mission of Williston Central School is to create empowered learners who have a clear understanding of and ownership for their learning, have a positive self-concept and global understanding, and who have acquired the behaviors and

skills to become lifelong learners. (Mission Statement, Williston Central School, 1994)

Williston was also attractive for its open outdoor spaces and recreational opportunities. The recreation field behind the school includes a smooth, paved path that is perfect for rollerblading and jogging. I would do laps on the path, which at the time was new and not yet discovered by the general population. There were days, especially during cold but dry weather, when I was the only person rollerblading and using the path. The town is also a nice starting point for bicycle riding through nearby towns such as Richmond, Jonesville, and Jericho, with rolling hills and magnificent views of the Green Mountains. My favorite training ride was a 12-mile loop out and back along the Winooski River that ended with a hill climb from the river to Williston town center, which is on a plateau. Williston also borders Lake Iroquois, which is perfect for kayaking. We had four kayaks, and I designed and fabricated a rack on a small-boat trailer that hitched to our car to conveniently transport the equipment. When we were all on the lake together, we looked like a family of ducks paddling in unison.

The house we built was in a new, nine-home development called Turtle Pond, within walking distance of Williston Central School. There was, in fact, a pond on the property, and each year at least one very large turtle would crawl out of the water. As the other homes were not yet built, except for one spec house still on the market, we were the first family to move into the neighborhood and we hoped the house would appreciate significantly since we bought in on the first wave. Turtle Pond gave us the opportunity to design a home based on our needs and what we had learned from living in three other houses. We lived for 27 years in that house at 10 Turtle Pond Road, and our adult children fondly remember it as the family home.

The house was built on a one-acre lot, which kept me busy maintaining our landscaping, mowing the lawn, and cutting back the perennially encroaching trees and natural shrubs. I approached these tasks as "meditations." I would say, "I'm going out to do the lawn-mowing meditation," an opportunity to put on a pair of noise-muffling headphones and have some outdoor time to myself. Our lawn was the envy of the community and eventually served as a pleasant location for events such as Kali's Bat Mitzvah celebration and a reception associated with Leah's wedding. I built a sandbox for the children when they were young, but unfortunately it was discovered by some outdoor cats. I also built a tree house for the children with monkey bars, a swing, and a ladder leading up to a small house with a shingled roof and arched windows.

Throughout a 15-year time period that included living in Essex, Jeffersonville, and Williston, I was practicing as a psychologist with offices in Essex Junction. I was a business partner with Marc and Judith, also psychologists and contemporaries with similar values and worldviews. As our practice grew, we took on two additional partners, one of whom was an intern I had supervised toward his psychologist license in Vermont. With a 20-page partnership agreement, we each bought shares in the company and we went on to build an office building for the practice. The lot we purchased had a decrepit old house that we tore down to make way for a 6,000-square-foot office building. We designed half of the building for outpatient psychotherapy with 10 therapy offices, a conference room, and a large open common space for patient reception and a waiting area. We left the other half open and rented it to another business.

Psychologists do not need a lot of medical equipment, but what we do need is privacy and confidentiality. Therefore, the most important feature in a therapy facility is soundproofing, a feature that any psychologist or therapist will tell you is difficult to achieve. In fitting up our building for therapy offices, we took pains to insulate the walls and install solid-core doors with carpet sweeps; we even added insulation to the acoustic ceiling tiles. The offices were desirable, and at our peak point we had 18 therapists working in the space, including the five partners.

But there were cracks in the partnership. As health insurance companies introduced "managed care," we were not always in agreement about how to cope with the intrusive threat. Managed care is an effort by health insurance companies, who pay for medical and mental health services, to control their expenses and maximize their profits. In the name of quality care, they began requiring therapists to obtain pre-authorization for counseling services. Furthermore, they would authorize only a limited number of visits before another authorization request was required. At first, one of the biggest insurers in Vermont would authorize only three visits before a follow-up treatment authorization request was necessary. The request forms were time-consuming and burdensome, and it was apparent that their motivation was to discourage longer-term therapy. By making the authorization process cumbersome, requiring telephone case reviews on patients needing extended care, and keeping the reimbursement rates level for years, the health insurance companies were quite clearly driven by the profit motive. Insurance companies were in a delicate dance between maximizing profits while avoiding lawsuits for denying care. This created a trust problem between providers and insurance companies, as well as stress on us as providers.

At one point, I went online to research the executive salaries of the health insurance companies with which we had provider contracts. The salary profiles were considered public information, and it did not take long to learn that numerous presidents and vice presidents were earning salaries in the *millions*. And those numbers did not include bonuses, benefits, or golden parachutes in retirement packages. It is one thing for health care to be a for-profit business, but it is another to make money at the expense of patient care and provider compensation.

Our business partnership was under pressure to cope with managed care, and our overhead expenses were outpacing our income. We were not in agreement about how to manage managed care, which some health care professionals were calling "mangled care." As conflict between the partners intensified, we reached a point of irreconcilability. Ultimately, we dissolved the partnership, and the practice was sold to a hospital as we went our separate ways. It was a painful and anxiety-arousing period, much like a divorce. Ironically, the hospital that purchased the practice asked me to stay on as the director, and I was offered an attractive salary. For the next two years, I was the director of the practice that I previously co-owned.

One of the ways my childhood trauma experiences affected me is how sensitive and resistant I am to feeling controlled by others, especially people in positions of authority. I have noted this in situations in which there are power differences between me and others, such as supervisors or managers above me. I also recognized this pattern as I reflected back on my conscientious objector case, where I was not willing to take orders in a war that seemed immoral and unnecessary. It takes a high level of respect and collaboration for me to be comfortable working under someone else's leadership, and I was not feeling it with my immediate superior at the hospital. Just as I was not happy working under a particular CEO at a mental health center in Bennington, I was unhappy with this employment arrangement.

Hospitals are by nature bureaucratic, and even though I was the director of the practice newly owned by the hospital, I was not comfortable reporting to a second-level manager in a bureaucracy.

I certainly know how to function effectively in organizations, and my colleagues would describe me as a team player, but I prefer to be my own boss. I can think for myself, and I do not want to be controlled professionally or personally by others. My pattern of resistance to authority was evident in other instances, such as participating in civil rights marches and antiwar demonstrations. Even my parents, before they divorced, modeled autonomy and truth to power. They were community organizers who created a co-op at the Amsterdam Houses. The resulting economic system bypassed the price markups at supermarket chains on basic goods such as milk, eggs, butter, flour, and sugar.

I knew in graduate school that I wanted to be in control of my professional life by establishing a private practice of my own. It took some 12 years working in hospitals and mental health centers to develop sufficient confidence, as well as to acquire the necessary business management skills. An opportunity presented itself when David Fassler, the psychiatrist and real estate investor I mentioned in Chapter 1, invited me to take an office in his premier waterfront building in Burlington. The building was on the aptly named Lake Street, and my office had large windows with views of Lake Champlain and the Adirondack Mountains across the lake in New York State. Looking out the window I could reflect on my childhood in New York from a more mature and accomplished viewpoint. I could see how far I had come from a traumatic childhood, when I was trapped and traumatized in an inner-city ghetto.

My new office was in a suite that evolved into the Vermont Center for Anxiety Care, the name I eventually gave to my practice. Another bonus was that the building was within walking distance of both the University of Vermont and Champlain College, as well as a short drive from Saint Michael's College, where referrals would originate.

The location was also just a few blocks from the Church Street Marketplace, a bricked-in promenade with restaurants, art galleries, and boutique shops. At the head of this gathering and shopping place was the magnificently restored Flynn Theatre. I would be working professionally in the heart of Vermont's cultural center, able to enjoy music and theater without the hassles of a big city like New York where I endured a traumatic childhood. It took 19 years and four houses to end up in Burlington, the city we eyed with envy when we first came to Vermont.

Years earlier, I got to know an elderly woman in Tennessee who lived alone in a house adjacent to the property purchased by MR and Tom. I visited her often and helped her with various maintenance tasks. She had a neuromuscular disorder that made it difficult for her to talk without resting her chin on the back of one of her hands. She spoke in a high-pitched voice, and I will never forget her favorite expression: "Well, if you don't have a dream, how are you going to have a dream come true?" I so resonated with that sentiment that I put it on our wedding invitations when Sheryl and I planned our wedding. Just as we designed our own wedding, we also designed the invitations, where I used my calligraphy skills to write the quotation inside a border of hand-drawn flowers. Reflecting on my life since moving to Williston and setting up my office in Burlington, I could say that I was living my dream. I had a successful private practice, an owner-designed home, and a beloved family with an angel soul mate and two amazing daughters.

When I left the hospital-owned practice to start my own business, I assembled a team of advisers and incorporated my practice. The team consisted of an attorney, an accountant, and a financial planner. Incorporating was consistent with my desire to own my own business and allow for control of my professional life. Within months of relocating my practice, I was on my way to creating the Vermont Center for Anxiety Care.

Several unique circumstances allowed me to expand beyond my solo practice and create a group practice and therapist training center. One was a shortage of child psychologists in Vermont; I was able to leverage the shortage into contracts with health insurance companies to permit supervised practice. This meant that unlicensed therapists could provide services under my supervision, resulting in a win-win-win outcome: Early-career therapists could acquire the supervised practice hours needed to qualify for their licenses in Vermont, I could get paid to supervise motivated therapists and influence the next generation of therapists, and more Vermonters could receive quality care. Clients who would otherwise go onto my waiting list could get help sooner if they agreed to work with therapists under my supervision. The vast majority of clients opted for this arrangement. Another unique feature was that only PhD psychologists and MDs could qualify to assume the supervision responsibility.

Word got out that therapists graduating from programs in psychology, clinical social work, marriage and family therapy, and mental health counseling—if interested in private practice—could receive supervision at the Vermont Center for Anxiety Care as required for professional licensure. In fact, many of my interns, as we refer to them, opt to stay on at the center because it is the very type of setting to which they aspire. This contrasts with the more typical path of working "in the trenches" for agencies and mental health centers before entering private practice. I, for example, worked for 12 years at three different community mental health centers before I had enough experience and confidence to enter private practice. At the Vermont Center for Anxiety Care, therapists could gain not only clinical experience but also business experience, which graduate schools do not include in their curriculums.

I focused on anxiety disorders as my practice "brand." I had already written my first book on the topic of anxiety, *Dancing With Fear* (1994), and I had begun to teach internationally on the topic. I knew that anxiety was, and still is, the number-one emotional disorder in the world. However, I wondered if an identity as an anxiety treatment specialist would limit the types of referrals and clients seeking help. It turned out to be the opposite: As the community recognized me as a specialist in anxiety disorders, they also asked about my expertise in other mental health conditions. Furthermore, since anxiety is embedded in almost all other mental health and medical conditions, I was considered a resource for help with a wide range of issues including depression, relationship problems, adjustment to medical conditions, retirement issues, child behavior problems, student academic difficulties, gender identity concerns, eating disorders, and so on.

I started the center by adding several therapists to my practice. My office was in a four-office suite, and within a year the space was maxed out with interns. To keep up with the demand for our services, I would need additional offices. When a seven-office suite became available in an adjacent building, I relocated the group. I remember hiring a moving company and watched with astonishment how the movers loaded a truck with our furniture, drove it across the parking lot, and unloaded the contents. This method was probably more efficient than carrying each piece of furniture by handcart or dolly across the parking lot.

The new office suite was unique in that it was in a historic mill building with original posts and beams and 14-foot-high ceilings. We hired an interior decorator to design the space for our needs as a psychology practice, and she proposed some stunning features such as glass partitions with powder-coated posts for privacy in child and adult waiting areas, green glass pendant lights, a granite reception counter, and tongue-in-groove cherrywood paneling on the common-area walls. For ambient music to help mask voices in the therapy offices, I added a sound system with four speakers installed high on the sand-blasted posts. Since there was plentiful sunlight pouring in through plexiglass transoms surrounding the common area, we filled the space with light-loving plants. The setup was classy.

As I added more interns to the center, we reached maximum capacity with the seven offices. I then took advantage of a suite that opened up on the second floor. The suite, which had nine offices, was formerly occupied by a mortgage company that had invested in ame-nities such as wood paneling and a nice reception area. We rehired the interior decorator to design the common area, which had a 14-foot-high ceiling similar to the downstairs suite. We duplicated the par-titions of etched glass and powder-coated posts for the waiting area, and we wired in a sound system for pleasing, noise-canceling music. We also took the designer's advice on wall sconces and pendant light-ing, as well as paint color for the offices. It was, once again, a classy yet relaxing professional office in a prime location on the Burlington waterfront facing Lake Champlain.

With time and further growth of the practice, we added an adja-cent suite with two offices and a large conference room. The addi-tional offices were at one time part of the suite we were already using. The additional offices all had eight-foot-high windows overlooking Lake Champlain and the Adirondack Mountains in New York State. Some people familiar with commercial real estate have remarked that we have the nicest offices in Burlington if not all of Vermont.

I wasn't entirely comfortable with my original name for the growing practice—the Center for Anxiety Disorders. The issue was with the word *disorders*. I do not think anxiety is an illness or even a disorder, but I could not for the longest time think of a way to modify the name. Walking past the signboard as they entered the suite of offices, even some clients expressed their dismay about being considered "disordered." I invited suggestions from my staff but none felt right until a remarkable event resolved the issue. I was teaching a workshop on anxiety to mental health professionals on Long Island, as I had done in the same community two years prior. At the end of the day, four or five psychologists approached me and handed me a pen. I initially thought they were gifting me a pen as a token of appreciation, but as they did, they said, "It's not about the pen." They explained that two years prior, I had inspired them to start a practice specializing in anxiety, the name of which was right there on the pen: Long Island Center for Anxiety *Care*. At that very moment a light flashed and a bell rang in my mind, and I thought, "That's it!" I could rename my practice, the Vermont Center for Anxiety Care. I took the name to my staff meeting and everyone immediately said, "Yes!" We all felt that the word *care* represented our value system about the healing work we do. I modified our logo and signage, updated our website, and ordered stationery with the new name.

Reflecting on our success, it is apparent that the most important ingredient has been choosing the right therapists for the practice. In interviewing candidates for therapist positions, I focus more on potential and the qualities that cannot be taught than experience in the field. While solid training and some experience is important in new hires, I am interested in qualities such as empathy, compassion, warmth, self-awareness, good verbal communication skills, a sense of humor, work ethic, eagerness to learn, and good relationship-building skills. Since therapists are the instruments of their healing art, we need to be tuned with these basic qualities. Also important is that therapists who work with me need to feel that this work is their purpose in life.

I know that if I pick the right people and offer them experience and individualized supervision, they can reach their potential and become exceptional therapists.

I have articulated the importance of choosing the right people in a document I give to all applicants for therapist positions at the Vermont Center for Anxiety Care. Printed below is the document I have entitled, *My Supervision Philosophy*.

Clinical and professional supervision at the Vermont Center for Anxiety Care begins with hiring post-degree interns who, in my judgment, possess the potential to become exceptional therapists. This includes personal qualities such as self-awareness, motivation to learn and grow, strong work ethic, effective verbal communication skills, compassion, high value on health/wellness, and interest in private practice.

The purpose of supervision is to support clinicians in achieving their potential through opportunities to practice the craft of therapy combined with my evaluative feedback, suggestions, and recommendations. To be successful, supervisees need to be proactive, assertive, honest, open, and courageous in reflecting on themselves and their clients.

My supervision philosophy is based on a model that was instrumental in developing my own therapeutic style. The model involves trusting and empowering supervisees to practice unattended within the walls of their offices, followed by discussion in supervision. At the same time, it is important to remember that cases treated under my license are legally and ethically my responsibility. Therefore, there may be occasions when I must step in and render unilateral decisions and instructions.

During the past 45 years as a licensed psychologist, I have served in numerous supervisory roles in settings such as graduate schools of psychology, mental health centers, hospitals, and private practice. I am committed to the psychology and counseling professions, and I take seriously the role of preparing early-career mental health professionals for the responsibilities inherent in serving the public as clinicians, consultants, educators, and researchers.

The orientation of my APA-approved pre-doctoral internship in clinical psychology at the Department of Psychiatry, Mount Zion Hospital and Medical Center in San Francisco, was psychoanalytic. My supervision orientation reflects this background in that I focus on issues of therapist countertransference, the importance of trust in the therapeutic relationship, the role of unconscious motivation underlying behavior, and the transformative power of insight and self-awareness.

During the course of clinical practice as well as research involved in writing several books on anxiety, I have added a cognitive-behavioral orientation to my work. In supervision I emphasize the importance of changing thought patterns and integrating specific skills in therapy. These include mindfulness, relaxation and stress management, good health habits (nutrition, sleep, exercise), and interpersonal/communication skills. In general, I believe that therapy is most likely to be successful when there are clearly articulated goals and a collaborative plan to achieve them.

My training included a practicum at the Vanderbilt Kennedy Center in Nashville, Tennessee, where I acquired a community and family orientation to clinical practice with children. I encourage my supervisees to view each client in a larger family and cultural context and to coordinate treatment with key resources such as parents, school systems, health care providers, and other agencies as appropriate.

My APA-approved doctoral program at Vanderbilt University in clinical psychology had a humanistic orientation that has influenced my therapy and supervision style. My supervisees are taught to respect each client's uniqueness and attend to individual strengths and capacities. I emphasize warmth, authenticity, active listening, and support in the therapy relationship.

As a psychology major at Yale University, I acquired a foundation in empirical thinking and published my first research study. My doctoral dissertation on cognitive styles was also published. These background experiences have heightened my respect for empirically based clinical practice. On the other hand, research on psychotherapy indicates that the therapeutic relationship is more important than empirical protocols and that no approach to therapy is more effective than others.

In supervision I encourage informal and formal assessment of therapy progress. This can be accomplished through rating scales as well as evaluation questions asked by the therapist at any time, such as, "Where would you say you are now on the journey toward your therapy goals?" or "How will you know when you have achieved your goals for therapy?"

I make sure my supervisees are fully informed about professional ethics as spelled out in the APA Ethical Principles of Psychologists. I encourage discussion of ethical issues on a case-by-case basis. In addition, I include discussions of state laws as they apply to counseling practice (e.g., duty to report and warn).

From a practical point of view, I meet with supervisees in regularly scheduled individual face-to-face sessions and weekly group supervision meetings. Methods of supervision include case presentations and discussion, clinical records review, review of and co-signature on outgoing correspondence, and observations of interactions with patients. Issues addressed include the following:

- *Standards for clinical* records
- Coordination of care with other resources (parents, schools, doctors, agencies)
- Diagnoses
- Treatment planning
- Countertransference issues
- Therapy styles and orientations
- Ethical issues in clinical practice
- State law as applied to clinical practice (e.g., duty to report, duty to warn)
- Business aspects of clinical practice
- Continuing education

During the same 20-year period that the Vermont Center for Anxiety Care was growing, I had an active speaking business. I traveled to teach, lecture, and conduct workshops to therapists, special education teachers, school counselors, classroom teachers, school administrators, and others. My most popular workshop focused on treating anxiety in children and adolescents. In addition to my book *The Worried Child* (2003), I went on to write a guidebook for therapists, *The Clinician's Guide to Treating Anxiety in Kids and Teens* (2017). *The Worried Child* was written for clinicians as well as the general public, whereas *The Clinician's Guide* was directed specifically to mental health professionals.

I traveled to an average of 30 cities per year, typically going on tour once a month to three cities. I have been to every state in the U.S., many more than once, and every Canadian province with just one exception. I had the good fortune of being invited all expenses paid to some amazing places, including Hawaii (three times), British Columbia (three times), Alaska (twice), Nova Scotia (twice), and some of my favorite states in the continental U.S., such as California, Florida, Arizona, and New Mexico. I visited cities like New Orleans, San Diego, San Francisco, Flagstaff, Albuquerque, Taos, Phoenix, Boulder, Vancouver, Halifax, West Palm, Minneapolis, Dallas, and many more. I even taught for a week at an international conference in Havana, Cuba. I would sometimes take Sheryl on my speaking trips when we wanted to add some extra days for sightseeing and vacationing. All told, I have taught at least 500 workshops and I have been on at least 600 airplane flights. For a victim of childhood abuse suffering from anxiety and shaky self-esteem, and who had no idea how to escape from Hell's Kitchen, I feel blessed to have found a way to travel and see the world.

There have been some interesting benefits to my speaking business. I ate the freshest salmon and king crab in Alaska, the best steaks in Omaha, and the freshest lobster in Maine and in Cape Cod, Massachusetts. For several years, I taught a one-week summer course at the Cape Cod institute, where my compensation included a home large enough to have my wife, Sheryl, our two daughters with their husbands and our grandchildren join me for one-week vacations. My speaking business also enabled me to get away from the long, cold winters in Vermont by accepting lecture invitations to Sunbelt states such as Florida, North and South Carolina, Texas, Arizona, New Mexico, and California.

I once got a job as a cruise lecturer. My category was "life enrich-ment," as distinct from cruise entertainment. In exchange for giving five one-hour lectures on board a cruise ship to the Caribbean, I could go on the cruise with Sheryl at no charge. On the ship I gave lectures on topics such as How to Stay Relaxed After Your Cruise Vacation; Meditation; Yoga for Beginners; and Stress Management Skills. We got hooked on cruises and we made it an annual ritual to book a cruise vacation to the eastern or western Caribbean. We visited the islands of Saint Thomas, Saint John, Saint Maarten, Antigua, Martinique, Puerto Rico, Saint Croix, Haiti, Saint Kitts, Jamaica, Saint Lucia, Barbados, Aruba, Cozumel, the Bahamas, and the Caymans, almost all of which had colorful street markets and amazing beaches. At some of the islands, the snorkeling was so colorful it reminded me of some of my psychedelic trips.

The speaking business dovetailed with my books and my clinical practice. As an author who had written four books on the subject of anxiety, I was considered an expert in the field. There was a synergistic relationship between my clinical practice, books, and the speaking business in that my clinical practice inspired my books, which gave me credibility as a speaker. The speaking business resulted in more book sales so that my income as a psychologist included therapy fees, speaker fees, and book royalties. In addition, some of my workshops have been recorded and they are sold as continuing education prod-ucts, further adding to my royalty income.

My speaking business took me all over North America but I never had a chance to teach in Europe. As a college student, however, I took an eight-week vacation to Europe paid for by a tax refund of just $250. I visited London, Paris, Amsterdam, Munich, Madrid, Venice, and other cities. I will never forget driving a rented Renault on the Ger-man autobahn, which has no speed limit. Even as I was driving at 120 kilometers per hour (85 mph), other cars would pass me so quickly that I did not see them in my rearview mirror and could hear them only as they flew past me. To make my meager budget last, I ate a lot of bread and cheese accompanied by an occasional tomato.

Although it was not a teaching trip, I was blessed to take that European ski vacation with Sheryl when our girls were old enough to spend a week at home with a babysitter. Lisa, an older adolescent with a driver's license, was like a big sister to our girls. I think we as parents had more difficulty separating from our girls than they did from us. Of course, we spent considerable time preparing the girls, and ourselves, for the one-week separation. I described the memorable ski adventure previously in Chapter 13.

We raised our two precious girls during our years in the Williston house, which they think of as their family home. After graduating from the Williston Central School, they moved on to Champlain Valley Union High School, the regional public high school that served several towns in the area. Leah joined the Nordic ski team and became vice president of her class; she went on to be the valedictorian of her graduating class. Kali came into her own in high school. She won the U.S. Institute of Peace essay contest and received the award in Washington, D.C. She also went on a school trip to Greece led by her English teacher. Kali became a member of the stage crew for high school plays and performances. After high school, both girls went on to college. Leah went to Emory University in Atlanta, Georgia, and Kali went to the University of Richmond in Virginia.

When my daughters were still in high school, a big challenge for me was how to pay for their college educations. When we saw a notice at the high school for an evening presentation by a college financial planner, we signed up. When we showed up for the presentation, we thought we were in the wrong place as we were the only parents there.

It turned out we were the only parents who showed up and we met Jack Trainham, a one-person business appropriately called College Financial Planning. I was naive and anxious about how to fund the girls' college education, and Jack helped us leverage the equity in our house as the source of funding. Subsequently, I invited Jack to be on my team when I incorporated my psychology business. Considering all that I have learned from him, there is no doubt that Jack has been an angel in my life. He is not only a financial genius, but he is also savvy regarding technology. I have consulted with him on purchases of computers, phones, iPads, helpful apps, presentation equipment, and even my television and home theater set up. I once told Jack that when I pay him for his services, I am actually reimbursing him for all the money he spends on trying out new technology.

There is one other thing I learned from Jack. Whenever I would walk into his office for a meeting or consult, he would greet me enthusiastically and say my name loudly, "Paul Foxman!" It seemed like he was always happy to see me and it made me feel special. As a result of those touching moments, I thought to myself, "I want all my patients and interns to feel that way when they have appointments with me." To this day, I greet everyone with whom I work with that same friendly and empowering enthusiasm.

Another financial challenge was to figure out how to pay for my two daughters' weddings. Again, Jack guided us in making it happen. We had two beautiful weddings, with live bands, good food, open bars, decorations, and memorable ceremonies. Both weddings took place at the Ponds at Bolton Valley, a picturesque setting nestled in a canyon on the access road to the Bolton Valley ski resort. The facility is a large, Adirondack-style building with a centrally located stone fireplace, overlooking a pond and Vermont's Green Mountains. With help from my friend Fred, I hand-cut some birch trees on his property and built a worthy chuppah, an open, four-post frame with cloth roof that is used in Jewish weddings to symbolize the home the newly married couple will build together. The history of the huppah goes back to the tent of Abraham, whose tent was open to hospitality. The huppah has no walls and symbolizes the openness to supportive relationships the couple will invite into their life together. The cloth covering represents the presence of God overlooking the covenant of marriage. The huppah we designed and made from natural materials is a work of art in which all the joints are numbered and the structure can be dismantled and reassembled with a drill and deck screws. We have lent the huppah to several other Jewish couples, and it has been used in both indoor and outdoor weddings. Fred and I both have high standards that border on perfectionism, and the chuppah we built is a masterpiece.

Kali and Leah were a joy to bring into the world and parent into adulthood. Unlike my family of origin, we were a close family with frequent expressions of love. We had no significant conflicts or behavior problems throughout their childhood and adolescence. It was a busy but smooth ride, and it was both painful and joyful to see them leave home for college. It did not occur to me that as they were getting older, so was I, and as they each left home for college, it slowly dawned on me that they were not necessarily coming back. They were moving into the next stages of life, hopefully prepared with strong foundations consisting of self-confidence, positive self-esteem, and high aspirations.

I miss my girls and I cannot go more than a month without a deep need to see them. When they were in college, we frequently drove the 650 miles to visit Kali in Richmond, sometimes just to see her compete on the crew team. I was stunned when Kali, who at home usually slept late on weekends and was not typically athletic, joined the crew team, which trained in the early morning starting at 5:30. And we traveled by air to visit Leah in Atlanta, which has the busiest airport in the country (Hartsfield-Jackson Airport has a four-stop underground subway). On some occasions we drove from Richmond to Atlanta after visiting with Kali, another 530 miles on top of the 650 miles from Vermont to Richmond. We put more than 100,000 miles on our car during those years: a pre-owned Volvo 650 Turbo station wagon with 5 cylinders that was referred to in a car magazine as "the 150-mph family hauler." The car's color, "Amethyst Metallic," was a deep purple, and it had flashy magnesium wheels that would appeal to anyone into cars.

Twenty-seven years in Williston is the longest time period of all the places where I have lived. In this chapter, I touched on some of my notable experiences and adventures in this location. But all things must pass, and after the girls were established in Boston with relationships and careers of their own, the time came for Sheryl and me to reevaluate our living situation. Leah obtained an MSW in clinical social work; she married Philip and started a family while she was working half-time with children at a mental health center. Kali moved up the ladder at a nonprofit organization and became the director of Jewish Boston, which I think of as the voice of Judaism in the Boston area and beyond.

As the girls were moving into their next stages of life, we became the cliché empty nesters. We no longer needed to maintain a large, aging house and property. I wanted the freedom to spend more time pursuing my personal interests and hobbies. This meant more time to play guitar, socialize, and enjoy outdoor recreation. I was not sure if I would be relieved or regretful living without the outdoor tools and equipment I acquired and learned to use proficiently. But after exploring options for a couple of years, Sheryl and I found an appealing opportunity in South Burlington, Vermont. The next chapter details my key experiences in this part of Vermont, where I still live.

CHAPTER 15

South Burlington, Vermont

(2012–)

SOUTH BURLINGTON IS A DENSE POPULATION CENTER, classified in Vermont as a city in contrast to the towns of Bennington, Essex, Jeffersonville, and Williston where we had lived. It is the third-largest city in Vermont, and the original headquarters of Ben & Jerry's Ice Cream. I would call South Burlington a suburb because it is primarily a residential and commuter community, although development is rapidly taking place, especially in the form of medical facilities, office buildings, and retail stores such as Trader Joe's and a Whole Foods–type health food store called Healthy Living, owned by friends of ours. South Burlington is also the home of Vermont's largest shopping mall. As part of rising residential development, we learned that a unique, "green agrihood" community named South Village was in the planning stages.

On 220 acres of conservation land, the plan was to build village-style, traditional single-family homes and townhouses while protecting 70 percent of the land from further development. South Village would be designated a chemical-free community with a working farm and preserved wetlands. At the time we discovered the South Village planned community, there were four flagship homes already built, but the project stalled because it was, I believe, ahead of its time. One of the single-family townhouses was the model home and was not occupied. It was used to display the available options and upgrades. The three-bedroom, two-and-one-half bathroom home had every conceivable option and upgrade, including a Viking kitchen with granite counters, a screened-in sunroom, large front porch, cement-board siding instead of vinyl siding, master bedroom on the first floor with two large walk-in closets, fireplace with tiled surround and fancy mantel, walk-in laundry room, upgraded wood floors on the main level, nine-foot ceilings with crown molding, solid-core doors, and built-in storage cabinets and bookshelves. The house even had a storage area above the two-car garage. The model home, built as a spec house by a couple we knew as cofounders of the Lake Champlain Waldorf School, was for sale. It was a magnificent home, but it was priced above our budget.

I came up with a bold and long-shot idea. I would not only offer the owner-investors of the model home a reduced price, but also make the purchase contingent on the sale of our Williston property. The real estate agent thought it was an unrealistic offer, as sellers are generally unwilling to take their property off the market for a risky contingency. I asked for 60 days to sell my house, after which the offer would be canceled. I secretly hoped our relationship with the sellers from our mutual Waldorf School days would move them to accept our offer. I was amazed and grateful when they did, and I thought to myself, "more angels in my life." The deal turned out to be low risk for the sellers, as our Williston house was under contract in less than one week. All the improvements and maintenance work we did on the Williston property paid off in the form of a significant equity jump that allowed us to afford the new home in South Village.

There was one concern we had about the South Village model home. As magnificent as it was, it was a townhouse sandwiched between two of the other flagship townhouses, and it received virtually no direct sunlight. The south side of the house, where maximum exposure to sunlight would normally occur, was the garage blocking the sun. Ever since my childhood summers in the Laurentian Mountains of Quebec, I have been connected to the outdoors and sunlight. I can always tell what time of day it is by the quality of light, even on cloudy days. And remember, my Indian name is Sun Dass—follower of the sun. In retrospect, we were so taken by the quality and magnificence of the model home that we went against our intuition that a home without direct sunlight would not work for us. Indeed, the model home in South Village darkened our mood, and it was not long before we realized we had made a mistake. It was even difficult to grow plants in the house because of insufficient sunlight. We realized we needed to sell the house and move on.

On top of that, I had developed a painful medical issue that is common in men as they age. To manage the pain, I was taking medication that affected my sleep, which in turn sapped my energy for exercising regularly as I was accustomed to doing for the previous 30 years. It took approximately two years to resolve the medical issue, but by then I had become deeply unhappy. The medical issue was another traumatic experience as well as my first mortality wake-up call, not counting the tracheotomy and two-week hospitalization at age nine.

We looked extensively at options for replacing the beautiful but dark home. It was a discouraging process but we persisted, driven by a sense of urgency. Then, to our delight, a new phase of development was planned at South Village that included a unique lot bordering the wetlands to the east and the farm to the west. We could situate a house on the lot that would take advantage of the open space and provide for a solar home. The developer's agent told us the lot would be ours when it became available. The promise was subsequently broken, and we learned the lot was under contract with another buyer. Our hearts sank, and this was the darkest point in our marriage. Miraculously, however, the lot became available when the other buyer backed out. When we learned about it, we immediately wrote a deposit check and Sheryl hand-delivered it to the agent's office. The building lot was ours.

Once again, we made the risky decision to build a new house before we sold our existing one. Going on faith, we began the process of designing the home we built and have enjoyed for the past five years. We incorporated everything we learned from our previous homes, especially the model home, and we paid special attention to the sun's arc. We included a lot of glass (41 windows), a deck facing the morning sun and conserved wetlands, solid-core doors with dark brass hardware, and nine-foot ceilings with crown molding. I wired the living room ceiling for a five-speaker surround sound system, augmented by a bass woofer that would be connected to the 56-inch flat-screen television that I would install above the tiled fireplace mantel. As cooking is one of my hobbies, we designed the kitchen with all the efficiencies we learned over the years. From my second-floor home office, I would be able to see eastward to Mount Mansfield, Vermont's tallest mountain, and westward to the Adirondack Mountains with the South Village Farm in between. We would wake up to the rising sun streaming through a huge picture window in the bedroom, and follow the sun throughout the day in the open floor plan. Designing a house is a blessing and although it is exhausting due to the many decisions that are involved, it is also exciting and rewarding.

Fortunately, the model home sold quickly and we timed the closing to coincide with the completion of the new home. We came close, but we needed to vacate the "old" house before the new house was ready for occupancy. We had a moving company put our household belongings into storage and headed off to Cape Cod where I taught my one-week summer course at the Cape Cod Institute.

One thing I have learned from buying and selling six homes in the 40 years since living in Vermont is that good fortune requires risk-taking. As a victim of childhood trauma, I have tended to minimize risk and avoid anything involving the unknown. I believe that taking risks requires trust and faith that things will work out. Victims of trauma generally have difficulty trusting and are oriented toward playing it safe. I had to learn to tolerate risks to be successful with home ownership as well as in business.

I was interested in solar power since the 1970s when the first iteration of solar panels was available. I told myself that someday I would have an efficient solar home. Within months after we moved into the new house, we contracted for the installation of a solar system. A reading of our solar orientation found that our roof would capture 92 percent of daily sunshine. The timing was fortuitous as the State of Vermont offered a 30 percent tax rebate of the total cost of a solar system. This is far more advantageous than a tax deduction. Furthermore, any excess electricity we would send to the grid would be purchased by the utility company at a higher price per kilowatt than we would pay if we needed to buy back some electricity if we needed more than we produced. On top of that, the state declared that towns could not raise the property tax on homes improved with solar power systems. The interest rate for solar power financing was low and tax deductible and, finally, any remaining loan balance could be transferred to a new buyer if the house was sold. It was a no-brainer, and I now proudly live in a solar-powered home with 24 solar panels on the roof that you cannot even see from the front of the house. For a person who was raised in a dark, sixth-floor apartment overlooking an unsafe truck route in Manhattan, this and my previous homes could be considered triumphs over traumas.

At the same time as I started a new phase of life by moving to South Village and eventually building the solar home, I started playing guitar again. Although I had stopped playing in graduate school to focus on my PhD dissertation, I knew in my heart that guitar playing would return at some point in the future. The "future" arrived in 2012 when I felt the inspiration and could make the time. My friend Fred had recently purchased a Martin guitar and had done the research on what was currently available. This saved me some time as I began my own quest for the perfect guitar. My criteria included a one-and-three-quarter-inch neck, which is slightly wider than typical, great sound, built-in electronics and tuner, and attractive appearance. It had to be something special to honor my return to playing music, as well as an investment in an instrument that typically gets better with age. I sampled many guitars and narrowed the search to a few models made by two popular guitar makers, Taylor and Martin. I was partial to Martin since it is an older company with which I was familiar. Martin also had a reputation for its distinctive sound made popular by contemporary professional players such as Eric Clapton and David Crosby (of Crosby, Stills and Nash fame).

The timing could not have been better when Jeff, the co-owner of the music store where I was sampling in-stock guitars, went on a buying trip to the Martin Guitar factory in Nazareth, Pennsylvania. He came back with a beautiful, one-of-a-kind guitar made in Martin Guitar's custom shop. From the first strum I knew it was the one. It has a neck made of European flamed maple, which I have never seen on any guitar before or since, a body made with exotic Bolivian rosewood with accents of mahogany, flamed maple purfling (joints between back, sides, and top soundboard), black ebony fretboard, brilliant pearl rosette surrounding the sound hole, built-in Fishman electronics, and a sunburst finish on an Engelmann spruce sound-board. It is not as flashy as some other high-end guitars, but it is clearly a work of art with a rich sound and long-lasting vibrato. I also purchased a Fishman amplifier to go with my fantasies of performing in public.

I have been playing guitar virtually every day since 2012, usually in the evenings, and my proficiency and artistry have grown dramatically. I also started to take voice lessons from a teacher who once complimented me by saying, "You're not supposed to be this good at your age!" Since I started playing again, I have been driving once each week to Jericho, Vermont, to play guitar with Fred. Usually on Saturday afternoons, we engage in uplifting spiritual conversation followed by a music session. In warm weather, we set up outdoors on his very private property and play from the top of a hill with trees behind us facing an open area, making for a remarkably effective, natural acoustic amphitheater. The visits have been the highlights of my weeks, and playing guitar again has proven to be therapeutic and a boost to my self-esteem. My confidence was high enough that I started playing in public. I got as far as performing one night at a restaurant in Stowe, Vermont, but then the coronavirus emerged and everything shut down. I have written the music and lyrics for 10 songs that I hope to record one day, and there are two other players already signed on to back me up.

How ironic that just as I have reached the pinnacle of my life and career, I would be derailed by a pandemic and health crisis that took me to the edge of death. After a lifetime of hard work, education, and life experience, I had reached a high point of security and success. In fact, just months before the genetic cardiomyopathy hospitalization, I had established a revocable trust, updated my will and advanced directive, and even chosen the cemetery where I would be laid to rest at the end of my life. My affairs, so to speak, were in order. Sheryl, ever the psychologist, said that I must have known something I did not know I knew.

Paradoxically, the pandemic has been a boon to my psychology practice. We cannot keep up with the demand for our services even though I have added more therapists to the staff at the Vermont Center for Anxiety Care. This seems to be true for mental health professionals nationally. While so many businesses have suffered or even folded as a result of the pandemic, our business has grown. It's a twist of fate that could never have been predicted.

This book is a life review and account of a journey from a traumatic childhood to a fulfilling, happy, healthy, and blessed life. If I were to die today, I would leave behind a legacy of having made a difference in the world. I have helped many people heal from their suffering—at least that is what people tell me. I will leave behind my wonderful children and their children, who call me "Papa." I will leave behind the Lake Champlain Waldorf School that I cofounded in 1985. I will leave behind a successful psychology practice and therapist training center, which I hope will continue to operate under new leadership. I will leave behind the books I have written on the topic of anxiety, hoping they will help therapists heal their clients and the general public overcome anxiety. And I will leave behind the many people whose lives I have touched and who have come into my life as angels without even knowing it. But I feel it is not yet my time. Besides, I have yet to record a music CD so that I can leave behind a piece of art that will resonate with those who may have a chance to listen.

In the final chapter to follow, I attempt to pull together and organize what I have learned about resilience, trauma recovery, and purpose in life. The final chapter is where I extract from my biographical story some of the lessons and insights that might serve an enduring purpose by helping others transform their traumas to triumphs. I cannot be the only one to have done this, and I hope many others will have the same gratifying experience.

CHAPTER 16

Reflections and Insights

MARK TWAIN WROTE, "The two most important days of your life are the day you are born and the day you find out *why*." One of the greatest blessings in my life has been to discover my purpose—what I was born to do—and to have a chance to live a life with meaning and purpose. I sometimes joke that it seems a shame to take a lifetime to understand why we are here and then miss a chance at another lifetime to benefit from the insights, understanding, and awareness it took a lifetime to learn. If I do not have another lifetime ahead, I would at least like to pass on what I have learned so that others can benefit and have more time to live on purpose.

In this book, I have shared and discussed the touchpoints of my life during the first 74 years. I wish I could have another 74 years, but at least I can say it has been an emotionally rich life so far and I feel proud of my accomplishments. What I have achieved goes far beyond what I could have imagined as a child trapped and traumatized in a ghetto for 18 years. What have I learned about resilience, trauma recovery, happiness, and success that I can pass on to you?

Some people say that recovery, success, and happiness begin with *hope*, but I say they begin with *belief*. In my mind, hope is more passive than belief. Hope is expressed as "I hope things will work out," and implies little control over what happens. In contrast, belief is expressed as "I believe things will work out," and signifies control, intention, and expectation. What you believe is possible has a significant impact on what you are able to achieve. If you believe that what you want in life is impossible, or that you do not deserve it, what would motivate you to do the work required to manifest your dreams? As my elderly, widowed friend in Tennessee said many times, "If you don't have a dream, how can you have a dream come true?" I am certain she was an angel in my life teaching me that my dreams could be realized. She reinforced the idea that you must not only have dreams, but you must also believe they can come true.

As a musically inclined person, I often find meaning and inspiration in songs, and there is a powerful song that speaks to the power of belief. The song *When You Believe*, from the DreamWorks animated musical *The Prince of Egypt*, was made popular by Mariah Carey and Whitney Houston. Although hope is referenced in the song, it is belief that underlies the miracles that can be achieved. Here is an excerpt . . .

> *There can be miracles*
> *When you believe*
> *Though hope is frail, it's hard to kill*
> *Who knows what miracles you can achieve?*
> *When you believe, somehow you will*
> *You will when you believe*

I have discovered that there are two forces or instincts operating within each of us. One is the survival instinct, the brain function whose purpose is to keep us alive. Mediated by the base brain (the same part of the brain that exists in all animals, including insects), the survival instinct operates through vigilance to threats and dangers. When threat or danger is perceived, sometimes through a sixth sense, a message is sent to the organism to escape. When escape is not possible, the second line of defense is to attack. The escape mechanism varies by species, and in humans it often takes the form of avoiding risks and holding back.

With humans, perception of danger is complicated by the brain's temporal lobe (the brain area associated with memory), which can misperceive threat or danger when it reminds us of past adversity. We remember the past and overgeneralize threat or danger based on reminders or cues of past trauma. This activates the survival instinct, experienced as anxiety or fear, prompting us to escape or avoid. Based on our time awareness, the survival instinct also tries to predict the future. When the outcome of an action is unpredictable, we tend to avoid taking the risk. We will hesitate to take risks even when it is in our best interest. We may feel anxious about entering relationships, starting a business, going to graduate school, taking a trip, or countless other life options. We should be grateful for the survival instinct but also recognize that it can hold us back from trauma recovery, life fulfillment, and happiness. When the survival instinct is overactive, we do not change or grow.

I refer to the other force within us as the *growth instinct*. The growth instinct is the basis for evolution, both cultural as well as personal. It is the impetus for self-improvement, to become better persons by learning new skills, solving problems, and facing the unknown. The growth instinct enables us to take the risks inherent in virtually all new endeavors, especially when we cannot be certain of the outcome. However, if the growth instinct outweighs the survival instinct, we may take too many risks and act impulsively. We may act before we think, and endanger ourselves physically, financially, or emotionally.

We need a balance between the survival instinct and the growth instinct. The two forces need to work together—to negotiate with each other—for us to succeed in life. As a psychologist, I sometimes introduce this concept to help people make life decisions, recover from trauma, and fulfill their potential.

Earlier in this book, I introduced Barry as one of the angels in my life. Barry had a creative and insightful perspective on life, and he developed a unique language that enables others to grasp his insights. He saw that there are two realities in life. One is the "onstage" dimension in which people are characters in the play of life without knowing that it is a performance. For the majority of people, the "stage" on which they live is the only reality, and they take it seriously. They have little self-reflectiveness, or ability to see themselves from the "outside." In psychology, we refer to this as a deficit in "observing ego." In contrast, "backstage" is the place from which we can see ourselves as playing various roles in "real life." To be "backstage" gives us the option to see that who we are is more than our roles in life. It is a timeless, neutral, and objective viewpoint from which to see that we can make choices about how we live—how we choose to play "onstage." This is what theater is all about: An actor plays a part onstage and after the performance resumes his or her identity as a person outside of the role played on the stage. Barry's insight synchronizes with William Shakespeare's observation: "All the world's a stage, / And all the men and women merely players; / They have their exits and entrances; / And one man in his time plays many parts" (*As You Like It*, Act II, Scene VII).

Using the theater analogy, Barry would say, "You are not who you think you are," meaning that you are so much more than the role you are playing in life. The person who cannot get backstage gets stuck in a limited, prescribed onstage role. Growth and change are not possible for those who are stuck in their onstage roles.

I believe this is one of the secrets of my success. Beginning early in my life, I have felt like a visitor from another planet or reality viewing life as an outsider. I am *in* this world but not *of* this world, a perspective that has allowed me to observe life objectively and choose what roles I play on the stage of life without losing my core sense of self. This has freed me to believe that anything is possible and that I have the capacity to overcome adversity and manifest my dreams.

Barry would also say, "If you're backstage, you don't age." I have never felt old, although I am aware of time and I see that the horizon is much closer now. If I pay attention, keep an open mind, and see life as a series of learning experiences, I can stay forever young. This perspective is expressed in a song by Bob Dylan, "It's Alright, Ma (I'm Only Bleeding)." Written in 1964 and described by Dylan's biographer as a "grim masterpiece," there is a pertinent line, "He not busy being born is busy dying." I interpret this as a message telling me that to live a long and satisfying life, I need to continuously learn and grow. I am young despite the effects of aging on my body, and I am always learning, growing, and renewing. There is no limit to what I can learn and understand. As Einstein put it, "We could never know it all." There is within me an inquisitive and playful youth in awe of the universe and the miracle of life.

In another Dylan song, we are offered a prayer for fulfilling our dreams and experiencing joy. Below is a pertinent excerpt from the song, "Forever Young," which is in my guitar-playing repertoire.

Forever Young
Bob Dylan

May you build a ladder to the stars
And climb on every rung

May your heart always be joyful
May your song always be sung

Dylan also recognizes the role of helpers—who I have been referring to as angels— on the journey to happiness:

> *May you always do for others*
> *And let others do for you*

As I mentioned previously, when I started playing guitar again in 2012, I also began writing my own original songs. One of them, "Please Don't Leave Me Now," speaks to one of the things I have learned about trauma recovery and happiness. Once again, the theme is the important role of helpers on the recovery journey. Here are the lyrics to the song:

Please Don't Leave Me Now
Paul Foxman

CHORUS

> *Please don't leave me now*
> *Please don't leave me now*
> *Please don't leave me now*
> *Now that I found you*

VERSE

> *I thought that to survive I must be strong*
> *Now I know just how I have been wrong*
> *I was so alone, now I need friends to see me through*

CHORUS

VERSE

> *I know that to be wise I must see*

How things are and how they need to be
I was lost and now I need to find my way back home

CHORUS

From time to time, I have been asked, "What is your secret for success and happiness?" and "How have you managed to accomplish so much in your life, including writing 4 books while working full-time, creating a thriving business, raising a family, exercising regularly, maintaining a home and property, and co-founding a Waldorf school?" On reflection, I am aware of three ingredients necessary to achieve fulfillment and an accomplished life, despite a trauma history. The first ingredient is *energy*. Energy is the raw fuel for getting things done, for doing the work required for achievement and success. Like solar energy from the sun, the universe provides unlimited energy if we know how to access it. One way to access energy is through health and wellness, and I believe we can define health in terms of energy. Healthy people are energized and vibrant, and their health is observable in the clarity of their eyes, the way they walk and move, their mood, and the way they make others feel in their presence. But energy is not a material substance. It is more like electricity: You cannot observe it directly, but you can see its effects as it powers an electric car or lights up a city. Energy has been called by different names, such as vital force, spirit, verve, vitality, vigor, stamina, potency, and drive. It is the electromagnetic force that keeps our heart pumping 100,000 times a day for a lifetime without a break and without a battery or wind-up mechanism. Energy is the life force that enables us to actively pursue our goals and dreams. The opposite of energy is apathy, laziness, lethargy, and inactivity, the qualities that interfere with success and happiness.

In my other books, I detail the lifestyle factors that contribute to health and energy. I point to three fundamentals of health: good diet, exercise (cardiovascular, strength, and flexibility), and restorative sleep. I will not go into more detail here, other than to say that health has been a high priority for me since adolescence. When asked about my priorities, I always say, "Love, health, and financial security, in that order." The payoff for my health and fitness is that it saved my life when I was recently hospitalized with genetic cardiomyopathy. My brother, Marc, who was hospitalized with the same condition, did not make it out of the hospital.

The second ingredient necessary for success is *efficiency*. Efficiency signifies a peak level of performance that uses the least amount of effort to achieve the maximum results. Efficiency requires reducing the number of unnecessary resources, such as personal time and energy, used to produce a desired outcome. Since efficiency is related to how we manage time, we can increase our productivity with time-management strategies. As a simple example, each time I go up or down the stairs in my house, I pause and ask myself, "What can I bring with me so I can avoid having to make two trips?" Another example is how I have organized my kitchen: The cutting board, knife rack, compost bucket, mixing bowls, food storage containers, plates and bowls, cutlery, trash, and sink are all within one step of each other. And I have trained my staff at the Vermont Center for Anxiety Care to use a digital calendar or spreadsheet for appointments that can contain all the information needed by our billing service. This avoids having to fill out a separate appointment log for the billing service to send claims and invoices to payers.

Being organized is another way to increase efficiency. If everything has a place, it takes much less time to retrieve a needed item, whether it's a nail clipper, #2 Phillips-head screwdriver, or filed information. Investing time in creating order and organization will increase efficiency and save time in the long run.

Planning ahead also improves efficiency. When I leave my house for a series of errands, I plan the route to minimize backtracking and I do my best to go out at times of low traffic and fewer crowds of people. Like many other people, I also prerecord television programs so I can fast-forward through commercial breaks. I have found that a one-hour television program is usually no more than 40 minutes of content, and by prerecording I can save 20 minutes as well as enjoy a program without interruptions. These are just a few examples of how thoughtful planning reduces wasted time and energy.

Whereas many people stress out about filing their annual tax returns, I use an electronic banking program for my business accounts. All the deposits and payments are recorded electronically and all my paperwork is filed in labeled hanging file folders. To provide the information needed by my accountant to prepare my returns each year, I simply upload my electronic files, as well as scan and securely email the necessary documentation. I have entered and filed everything during the course of the year so that the year-end process is efficient and painless.

One of my efficiency mottos is, "Why wait until tomorrow if you can get it done today?" I know that I am not likely to have any more time tomorrow than I do today. In addition, whenever possible, I do things while they are on my mind so I can avoid taking time to put them on a to-do list or trying to remember them.

I also find that I am more efficient by having routines and rhythms in my daily life. For example, over the years I have chosen gyms based on their location so I can exercise on the way to work. On three days each week, my routine involves exercising and showering at the gym and showing up at work refreshed and energized. When I used a gym with no towel service, I put a fresh towel in my gym bag and restocked depleted toiletries as soon as I came home from work. My gym bag is always ready to go and I don't forget the fresh towel or other items.

I can think of dozens of other efficiency routines. One is to recharge my bicycle accessories, such as lights, electronic shifters, and a wireless communication helmet, when I return from a ride so the bicycle is always ready to go. Yet another time-saving routine is when I cook a meal (cooking is one of my hobbies), I always make enough food for a second or even third meal, such as a lunch, snack, or dinner later in the week. To me, efficiency is a matter of common sense, time-management, and mindfulness.

We tend to be more motivated when there is a sense of urgency or awareness that time is limited. It helps to keep in mind that the average lifetime is 78.54 years in the U.S, and an astounding amount of that time is spent on basic needs and necessary tasks that do not translate directly into happiness or lasting achievements. Most adults spend approximately one-third of each 24-hour day in bed, followed by paid work or school, housework, cooking and eating, driving, waiting in line or on the telephone with automated customer service, toileting, getting dressed, and leisure and stress-recovery (such as watching television). Together these activities take up 80 to 90 percent of the 1,440 minutes that we all have available every day. Parents with young children may have even less discretionary time due to taking care of their childrens' needs as well as their own. On a lifetime basis most of our time is accounted for, leaving little time available for self-improvement, making a difference in the world, or accomplishing anything of enduring value. The point is not to be discouraged by how little time is available for achieving long-term goals, but to realize that efficient use of time is necessary for accomplishing anything more than keeping up and getting through.

Carl Jung, a psychoanalyst and one of my virtual mentors, was interested in working only with patients who were at least 38 years old or, at minimum, seriously committed to the work of self-improvement.

His explanation was that until we reach the threshold of middle life, we have little sense of urgency and mortality. Before middle age, we can deceive ourselves into believing that the future is wide open and that we have plenty of time to accomplish our goals in life. However, as we become aware of the early signals of aging such as those telltale gray hairs in men and women or receding hairline in men, our motivation to make the most of our lives becomes more urgent. At that point we become more interested in addressing our personal symptoms of stress, depression, anxiety, lack of fulfillment, relationship discontent, and other obstacles to a well-lived life. When we awaken to the passing of time, our willingness to do the work of living fully reaches a new level of commitment. Our symptoms are a wake-up call to address the underlying suffering and, therefore, our suffering is a gift that points to the possibility of happiness and fulfillment.

Time is fleeting, and if we are not efficient or manage it wisely, we will be disappointed in what we can accomplish in a lifetime. A song entitled "Dust in the Wind," made popular by a legendary rock band named Kansas, who produced eight gold albums and was on Billboard charts for more than 200 weeks in the 1970s and 1980s, recognizes this truth. Here are a few relevant lines:

Dust in the Wind
Kerry Livgren

All my dreams
Pass before my eyes
All they are is dust in the wind

All we do
Crumbles to the ground, though we refuse to see
Nothin' lasts forever but the earth and sky

And all your money won't another minute buy
All we are is dust in the wind
Everything is dust in the wind

I discovered one of my secrets for happiness in a Chinese fortune cookie that read, "The secret to happiness is to enjoy what you have to do." If we can enjoy the daily tasks that otherwise might feel burdensome, we do not have to wait for our favorite activities to experience joy. For example, I have found that I enjoy what I need to do by using quality tools. I use a nice, one-of-a-kind pen that was hand-crafted by an artist I met in Hawaii. The pen is made of wood and acrylic, the same material used in making surfboards, and it sparks joy and fond memories when I use it. I have a set of quality knives that I enjoy using in the kitchen. I eat my breakfast cereal in a bowl handmade by an artist I met at a craft show.

I have also increased my happiness by transforming some daily tasks into mindfulness practices. I do them not just to get them done, although sometimes that is necessary for efficiency, but as opportunities to pay attention, slow down, and enjoy some of my daily tasks. For example, each evening before I go to bed, I use my oral hygiene routine as a mindfulness practice. Instead of rushing through this self-health task, I thoroughly floss and then brush for the full two minutes recommended by the American Dental Association. I use teeth-brushing as an anchor or focal point for my attention, and I let everything else go. In other words, my oral hygiene routine is a form of meditation.

Why have I chosen dental hygiene as a mindfulness task? For a number of years in Williston, I had a neighbor, a retired chemist, who managed a toothpaste manufacturing plant in Malaysia. She told me that one of her jobs involved research on how long on average people take to brush their teeth. This information was important to determine the amount of active ingredients to include in the formula based on exposure time—the amount of time consumers take to brush their teeth. She found that people invariably overreport the time they take. When timed in a test lab, people spend significantly shorter times brushing their teeth than they report in advance. People generally rush through their dental hygiene routine at the expense of thoroughness and enjoyment.

The third ingredient for living a productive and satisfying life is *focus*. Focus is sustained attention, the ability to keep an eye on a goal in the face of the many distractions that compete for our attention. People tend to start projects but not see them through because their focus is derailed by the countless distractions that call for attention and use up energy. It is easier to start than to continue, and to keep going requires the ability to maintain focus. One of my strategies for sustaining focus is to visualize a goal or finished project, and then work backward in planning and executing the steps needed to get from here to there. I also keep the goal in focus by taking at least one step daily toward the goal, even if it's only a small step. For example, when writing a book, I may take a simple step on an otherwise busy day, such as looking up a reference or reading something related to the book. In other words, I not only visualize the end product, but I keep the project alive and in focus by taking small steps until I have time carved out for more dedicated effort.

To maintain focus, it is necessary to distinguish between what is *important* and what is *urgent*. Some tasks have deadlines, but they do not connect directly to a person's long-term goals. For example, paying bills on time is driven by deadlines that do not translate into successful completion of long-term goals (other than financial solvency). Those tasks should be automated so that they are handled efficiently while maintaining focus on important, long-term goals.

Stephen Covey, a time-management expert who wrote the best-selling book *The 7 Habits of Highly Effective People* (1989), has created a four-quadrant matrix for distinguishing between importance and urgency. This framework can contribute to successful completion of long-term goals, such as personal development, trauma recovery, and life satisfaction. Everything we do can be put into one of the four quadrants or categories of activities proposed by Covey:

Quadrant I.   *Urgent and important*—important deadlines and crises that need attention

Quadrant II. *Not urgent but important*—long-term development and life satisfaction

Quadrant III. *Urgent but not important*—distractions with deadlines that should be delegated or automated

Quadrant IV. *Not urgent and not important*—frivolous distractions to be eliminated

Covey's research has found that people who rate themselves as happy and satisfied spend time regularly engaging in Quadrant II activities. These are the activities related to personal, long-term goals, or what could be described as, "what is important to *you*." Once we are clear about what is personally important, Covey advises that we *begin with the end in mind*, as well as *do the most important things first*. An example in my case is the importance of health. I invest time in regular exercise, eating well, and getting enough sleep.

Meditation practice is a singularly effective way to improve focus. The very process of meditation, as I have discussed earlier in this book, involves focusing on an anchor for attention and continuously refocusing on that anchor when thoughts go astray. The anchor for attention can be a meaningful word, a sound, or an object at which one gazes.

This practice trains the brain to develop the skill of sustaining focus in the face of distractions. I am certain that my meditation practice has enabled me to accomplish many goals and manifest many of my dreams. I practiced meditation earnestly for a long time beginning in San Francisco when John, my housemate and one of the angels in my life, taught me the proper steps. After some years of practice, meditation became more than a practice. Meditation became of way of life for me, a mindful way of being in the world.

I studied and experimented with two forms of meditation as part of my healing journey. One is *transcendental meditation*, which has its origins in Hinduism and which is connected to my yoga practice. The other is *vipassana*, also known as insight-meditation, which has its origins in Buddhism. So how can meditation help us to overcome trauma and adversity?

Legend has it that some 2,500 years ago, a privileged Indian prince named Siddhārtha Gautama seeking to understand the cause of human suffering left his wife and family to sit in meditation under a Bodhi tree in an area now known as Nepal. Vowing to meditate until the question was answered, he emerged six years later with four simple yet powerful insights that he taught as the Four Noble Truths. Siddhartha was subsequently named the Buddha, meaning "awakened one," and these insights have become the foundation of a now-popular philosophy of life, a sophisticated psychology of the mind and a method used in trauma recovery.

The First Noble Truth is that suffering is inevitable in life. The Second Noble Truth is that suffering is caused by *attachment*, meaning the impulse to hold on to the good and avoid the bad. The Third Noble Truth is that suffering can be overcome through *wisdom*, or understanding how to be with our thoughts and feelings without judgment and to be neutral or curious without craving the good or rejecting the bad. Buddhism teaches that we have a choice in every moment but that this requires awareness of our thoughts and feelings and the ability to witness them objectively.

This truth dovetails with one of the most popular psychotherapy frameworks of today, namely cognitive behavioral therapy. This approach to therapy is based on an idea formulated in the 1980s by Aaron Beck, Albert Ellis, and David Burns, known as "cognitive therapists." The idea was that how we feel is determined primarily by what and how we think. For example, worry thinking makes us feel anxious, and negative thinking makes us feel depressed. This premise evolved into a therapy approach that focuses on changing what and how we think. Since this is essentially the message of the Third Noble Truth, we could reasonably argue that cognitive behavioral therapy is a modern derivative of ancient Buddhism.

The Fourth Noble Truth emphasizes meditation as a path to overcome emotional suffering. For dealing with the pain of trauma or abuse, no practice is as beneficial as sitting still and learning to be at peace with ourselves in each present moment. Meditation grounds us in the present rather than what took place in the past or what may take place in the future. With such practice, we realize that feelings, memories, and even physical sensations are all temporary.

Following my heart failure trauma, which included 12 days in the hospital intensive care unit, I met with the cardiologist who managed my inpatient care. In the meeting, he made a point of telling me how impressed he was with the control I exhibited over my parasympathetic nervous system. In other words, he was complimenting me on how I kept my cool on the threshold of death. I attribute my calm state of mind and body to my meditation practice, which among other benefits has desensitized me to the quiet emptiness associated with the idea of death. During meditation we experience silence, stillness, and detachment. We "die" each time we enter this state and enter the timelessness behind thoughts. The more accomplished we become at this, the more comfortable we can be with our mortality. Meditation turns out to be good practice for dying.

Meditation, of course, does not prevent death, but it can counteract the *fear of death*. By practicing silence and detachment, we find ourselves in a simulated death state where we aim to do nothing other than to experience the quiet, empty space between thoughts. If I had to guess what death is like, that sounds like it.

Meditative practices involve a psychological mechanism called "interoceptive exposure," whereby we confront the sensations of a feared experience in order to master it. By sitting still and doing nothing, we are, in effect, confronting our trauma experiences. The exposure phenomenon in meditation "desensitizes" us to the emotional pain associated with having been abused, violated, or traumatized in any way.

Meditation also contributes to happiness by cultivating peace of mind. An agitated person who is not at peace is unlikely to be happy. According to the Dalai Lama, the acknowledged world spokesperson for Buddhism, happiness is a birthright as well as the goal of life.

The Buddhist assertion that happiness is life's goal synchronizes with a recent movement in my profession known as positive psychology, defined as the scientific pursuit of optimal human functioning. In this approach, it has been found that physical health and mental health can be enhanced by positive emotions, such as optimism, hope, gratitude, compassion, and awe. One finding is called the undo effect: Positive emotions seem to undo the physiological effects of stress, including trauma, and lead to greater happiness as well as better health and longer life.

At the same time, meditation helps us appreciate our aliveness. By focusing on a single point, such as breathing, a nature sound, or a special word or phrase, meditation sharpens our powers of concentration. This allows us to experience life more fully and with greater sensitivity. We become more able to engage in our moment-to-moment experiences, and as long as we are alive and well in the now, there is no death. There is only life *or* death.

One of my psychology interns at the Vermont Center for Anxiety Care has a sign in her office with a quote from a poem, *A Servant to Servants*, by Robert Frost: "*The best way out Is always through.*" This simple statement suggests that to heal from a traumatic experience, to get "out," we must face and process the ordeal. This is the essence of the Buddha's Four Noble Truths. In psychotherapy, we support clients in facing their trauma symptoms and memories and in moving through them in order to desensitize and heal. In the same way, meditation is a *sitting-with process* that can help us face and move through emotional suffering to healing and recovery.

Meditation is not the only recommended practice for overcoming the effects of trauma. As I mentioned in the Introduction, the mental health field now recognizes the importance of body work for trauma recovery. As a coping mechanism, trauma victims tend to disconnect or dissociate from feelings and physical sensations. In managing the impact of trauma, we may become numb and out of touch with our bodies. To recover from trauma, we may need to "reinhabit" our bodies and find ways to feel comfortable, competent, strong, and safe. In this recent somatic therapy approach, the recommendation is to engage in physical activities that activate the neural system that has shut down in response to trauma. High on the list of recommended activities are yoga, dance, playing music, and martial arts.

I was intuitively drawn to yoga while studying Eastern religions in my 20s. At the time, the connection between yoga and trauma recovery was not widely recognized. However, yoga meshed with my overall value on health and wellness, and I quickly discovered that through yoga I could feel relaxed and safe. I did not immediately realize that practicing yoga was actually repatterning my overactive nervous system. In the calm and relaxed state brought about by yoga, I became more able to stay focused on the present moment rather than on recalling the past or projecting into the future.

I now realize that the physical activities I enjoy, such as yoga, playing music, skiing, bicycle riding, kayaking, exercise, and even my love of using tools for repair and maintenance, have all contributed to my trauma recovery. All of these interests have served to connect me with my body, feel competent, and experience the healing power of creativity and nature.

I also discovered a healing state known as *flow*. Flow is defined as being engaged in an activity to the extent that one loses track of time and becomes one with the activity. But to experience flow, one needs to have enough skill or proficiency in the activity to experience joy and perform gracefully. To experience flow, one has to overcome the initial, and sometimes cumbersome, learning curve in an activity. Flow is predicated on practice and skill development. There must be an optimal match between the skill level of the person and the challenge level of the activity. Insufficient skill results in frustration, while boredom results when skill exceeds the challenge. This applies to virtually all activities, including art, cooking, yoga, meditation, skiing or snowboarding, bicycle riding, horseback riding, exercising, dancing, and playing a musical instrument. Anyone with skills in these activities will agree that they enjoy the experience most when they are focused but relaxed. Flow heals through an alternative state of being in which joy or exhilaration replaces anxiety and tension. It is virtually impossible to be anxious and in flow at the same time.

Flow is also good for self-esteem, as it can be associated with experiences of competence and mastery. In the Introduction, I referenced low self-esteem as a common consequence of trauma and a barrier to recovery and happiness. Low self-esteem handicaps people when it comes to dealing with life's curveballs and challenges. Low self-esteem causes us to personalize the adversities, insults, and frustrations in life. Lacking confidence to push back, stand up to, and prevail in the face of suffering, people with low self-esteem function as victims of life, unaware of their power. Furthermore, due to living in a culture largely disconnected from nature, many people are out of touch with their survival instincts and animal nature hardwired for resilience and perseverance. They do not know their true nature, and therefore they do not know that they are not who they think they are.

Under normal circumstances, there are two sources of high self-esteem. One is positive input from primary caregivers, preferably received early in development and internalized. Praise, love, attention, and caring translates into feeling "esteemed," into feeling valued, lovable, and worthy. Unfortunately, I did not receive much in the way of positive input as a child, largely because my father was absent and my mother was preoccupied with survival and raising three boys as a single parent.

On the other hand, I had the good fortune of having had many relationships with those who I have been referring to as "angels," a variety of people who supported me in so many ways and taught me so many things. These angels compensated for the first source of high self-esteem—positive input—and I am grateful for their love, support, and esteem-enhancing messages. In many cases, they were not aware of their positive impact on my trauma recovery, personal growth, and accomplishments. These relationships attest to the importance of social support on the recovery journey. Going it alone is not the way to go.

Psychotherapy is a special example of help and support for trauma recovery. I have been helped by several therapists, beginning with the experience I described in Chapter 1, when I was 10 years old and feeling guilty, angry, and sad about my parents' breakup. The second helpful therapy experience was my training analysis with Saul Neidorf when I was a psychology intern at Mount Zion Hospital in San Francisco. In Chapter 6, I discussed my relationship with Saul and how it allowed me to disclose for the first time the horror of my childhood abuse experiences. I sought support again in Nashville during my PhD program to address my fear of being alone and my need for social support. More recently, when I was dealing with a medical issue that brought my mortality into focus, I again sought therapy. All of these therapy experiences supported me through times of challenge as well as contributed significantly to my trauma recovery. By its very nature, psychotherapy also helps foster self-esteem. It is almost inevitable to feel valued and worthy when someone you trust treats you respectfully and with what we, as therapists, call *unconditional positive regard.*

The other source of high self-esteem is experiences of success, mastery, and accomplishment. These can include learning new things, developing new skills, and solving problems. But victims of trauma tend to avoid risk-taking, as their brains are wired for emotional or even physical safety. This can become a self-reinforcing cycle: Avoidance of experiences that promote high self-esteem results in fewer opportunities to develop high self-esteem. Furthermore, high self-esteem is not a static quality. It needs to be reinforced through repeated positive input from others as well as ongoing experiences of success, competence, and mastery.

In addition to social support and angel messages, my shaky self-esteem improved in adolescence and adulthood primarily as a result of competence and mastery in sports, academics, music, and tradesman skills. Discovering my aptitude in sports, for example, was an empowering source of self-esteem. My success as an athlete included being chosen as captain of my high school track team, as well as being recruited by the Olympic track coach at Yale. I was also a good student who experienced success in the form of high grades and GPA. As described earlier in the book, I also developed competence in the many skills I acquired in various summer jobs, the skills I used as a homeowner in adulthood.

A good sense of humor also helps with trauma recovery and happiness. Trauma activates a survival state, robs us of playfulness, and leads us to take life too seriously. A sense of humor involves stepping outside of ourselves and seeing with lightness the ways we try to cope with adversity. Laughing at ourselves helps us "lighten up," have fun, and experience joy. These positive emotions are helpful for tension release, stress management, and improved mood. Research has found that the muscles involved in simply smiling, let alone laughing, activate the release of feel-good hormones. We can actually feel better just by smiling, but laughing takes us all the way.

Finally, I have found personally and professionally in my work as a psychologist that a spiritual perspective is extraordinarily helpful for overcoming the damaging effects of trauma. Spirituality does not require any particular religious affiliation, just a belief in a higher power or intelligence. You could even be a naturalist, as was my mother, who believed that there is a natural order to life. For a long time, I could not grasp why I had been victimized as a child. If God exists, I wondered, why was I be a victim of abuse? In an effort to understand why I was victimized as a child, I studied religion in college and read the holy books of the world's most prominent religions—the Christian Bible, the Muslim Koran, and the Hindu Bhagavad Gita. Maybe there is a higher plan that accounts for violence, brutality, and trauma in the world, or maybe God gave man free will which can be so readily perverted and abused. I remember a funeral for a young woman who was raped and murdered: The presiding priest began by saying, "God is very sad today." That statement suggested that it would not be God's will for humans to be violent and barbaric. I have come to the conclusion that even if everything happens for a reason, we do not always get to know the reason. I realize that what we do with our adverse experiences determines what impact those experiences will have.

I also know that healing and happiness come from transforming trauma into purpose. When I experience adversity, I ask myself, "Is there a message for me in this experience?" In other words, I reflect on whether there is some kind of divinity involved. I began this book during my most recent trauma, a medical crisis that took me to the edge of death. In order to recover, I had to change my work-life balance. I had to stop seeing clients for an undetermined amount of time and limit my work to administration to keep my practice going. I had to cancel my scheduled speaking engagements and all travel plans. I pared down my work commitments to supervising my staff therapists and running my weekly case conference. On reflection, I realize that without the medical crises, I would not have slowed down or cleared more time for writing, playing guitar, and investing in my friendships. Considering that I had just reached a point where I could begin to implement a gradual retirement plan, it is quite possible that the medical crisis occurred for a good and higher reason. My recent medical crisis may have been divinely timed for my own best interest. If I recover successfully from the life-threatening heart trauma (and it seems to be going in that direction), I may actually end up grateful for the crisis.

It is impossible to know if I would have accomplished as much in my life had I not been traumatized and abused in childhood. But this much is certain: My adverse childhood was the driving force for making the most of my life. There seems to be a connection between my trauma history and my life purpose. My traumatic childhood equipped me for empathizing with and helping other people. I somehow gravitated toward a healing profession with a specialty in anxiety, and it has been a successful and rewarding career. It has been a blessing and an honor to contribute to the healing and personal growth of others, as well as to supervise other dedicated therapists for whom this work is also their purpose and calling.

I end this book with a startling but, in my case, applicable quote from *Legacy of the Heart: The Spiritual Advantages of a Painful Childhood* (Wayne Muller, 1992):

> I realize that it requires a tremendous leap of faith to imagine that your childhood—punctuated with pain, loss, and hurt— may, in fact, be a gift.

Scan the QR code for online recordings of some of the author's guitar music and original songs.

Index

CPSIA information can be obtained
at www.ICGtesting.com
Printed in the USA
BVHW041803090522
636560BV00002B/2/J

9 781684 428250